Dogs & Puppies

Dogs & Puppies

edited by DOUGLAS JAMES

with contributions from
Wendy Boorer
Judy de Casembroot
Alan Hitchins
John Holmes
Mary Holmes
Howard Loxton
Margaret Osborne
Mary Roslin-Williams
and Barbara Woodhouse

LONGMEADOW

Contents

First published in the USA 1977 by
Longmeadow Press, PO Box 16
Rowayton Station, Norwalk
Connecticut 06853

© 1977 Octopus Books Limited

ISBN 0 7064 0630 3

Produced by Mandarin Publishers Limited
22a Westlands Road,
Quarry Bay, Hong Kong

Printed in Hong Kong

The dog by man's side

There are hundreds of different breeds of dog known around the world. Some of them are rare, and restricted to a relatively small area, but many have travelled with man on his nomadic wanderings, his journeys of trade, conquest and colonization, so that they are now recognized and loved in many countries. Today the ease of modern travel enables the jet-age man to satisfy his wanderlust with speed and little physical effort. More people travel farther, and you might expect the modern dog to share in this increased mobility – but other forces are against it: frontier livestock regulations, disease restrictions, quarantine laws and the price of the dog's fare have to be taken into consideration. While man may jet across the oceans the dog, who always used to be at his master's heels in days of less sophisticated travel, is now more likely to be left at home.

In the past, when the world was a less organized place, the dog followed, or was taken, on many curious journeys for many curious reasons. Much of the early history of different dog types is very speculative, but we know that from the time the dog first took up with man the hunter a process of development and selection has taken place that has produced dogs equipped for a wide range of different tasks. The fluctuations of various breeds in different parts of the world throughout recorded history brings to light some fascinating anomalies.

For nomadic people the dog was a very important domestic animal, acting both as a guard and as a herder of their livestock, which crossed the world with them. The Dingo, for instance, is believed to have reached Australia as a fully domesticated dog in the canoes of the Aborigines. Once on the Australian continent, the Dingo became feral and soon contributed to the extinction of the less efficient marsupial carnivores.

The Maoris of New Zealand also arrived to settle in their islands with dogs in their canoes. They held their

dogs in high esteem, as is shown by the plume of dog's hair which decorates the carved staff of office of a Maori chieftain. The Maoris believed that when their ancestors were lost at sea or cast ashore on uninhabited lands without provisions, they might have to resort to cannibalism to survive but they would keep their dogs which would both warn them of danger and protect them from the perils of the unknown land.

From the Mediterranean Basin comes another breed of dog, greatly valued by the Bedouin tribesman, its original nomadic guardian and master. This is the Saluki, a breed of greyhound that has been known to the desert peoples since 5000 BC. The Bedouins had a general disdain of domestic animals but took a tremendous pride in their Arab horses and their Saluki dogs. They were allowed to share the Bedouin tents and the puppies were reared by the women of the tribe. On their longer treks the young animals were carried on the backs of the camels to protect their feet from the burning sand. Salukis were used primarily for hunting the desert gazelle, but they also caught smaller game and a well-trained Saluki can stalk a desert partridge and catch it in the air as it rises in startled flight. Like many animals held in high honour by their princely owners, Saluki were never sold, only given as gifts to those whom their masters wished to honour. For this reason it was not until the twentieth century that the Saluki became widely known in the Western world.

Another of the Eastern hounds, the Afghan Hound, is now better known in the West than in its native land. This breed is presumed, although on less evidence, to have originated in the Middle East with the other gazehound breeds. It could have reached Afghanistan with the camel caravans along the spice and silk routes to India. The Afghan tribesmen, who valued it for its hunting abilities, believed it to be indigenous to them so that, if the original migration did take place, it must have been extremely early in their history. Like the Bedouin, the Afghans were very jealous of their dogs and did not part with them lightly. However, when India was part of the British

This painting by Dürer shows the type of hounds used for hunting the stag in the fifteenth century. The hounds found and held the stag at bay, but were not expected to kill it.

7

Empire there were constant frontier skirmishes in the Himalayas and during the 'Afghan wars', in the latter half of the nineteenth century, British officers saw and coveted these dogs. It is likely that the breed's hunting ability first attracted their notice, since many army officers were devoted sportsmen. In ones or twos Afghan Hounds were taken back to Europe by their new masters, but they did not really make any impact on the dog world until the 1920s, when a number were imported from Kabul to Britain by Mrs Mary Amps. These, and a few other imports, were the foundation stock for the Afghan as it is known throughout the world today.

British army officers also introduced the German Shepherd Dog to England. They had seen them at work on the battlefields of the First World War, and when hostilities ended German Shepherds were taken back to Britain, and to America, by returning servicemen. In Britain a curious reversal in the breed's name took place: as there continued to be a great prejudice against all things German, the name of German Shepherd was dropped and they were first introduced as Alsatian Wolf Dogs. Thus a breed, which had first been distinguished for its qualities as a sheep herding dog, became known in Britain under a name associating it with the most feared predator of the flocks its forebears guarded.

The Doberman Pinscher was another guard dog taken home from Germany by soldiers after the First World War and introduced to America. The ears of this breed are cropped in its country of origin, which proved no obstacle in the United States where cropping is allowed. However, it contributed to the slower acceptance of the Doberman in Britain where cropping has been banned since the late nineteenth century.

One of the latest breeds introduced to America by returning servicemen has been the Akita. The American army of occupation in Japan met the Akita in its modern role as police and guard dog. The Akita is the largest of the three Spitz-type breeds to be found in Japan. Males can be up to 69 cm ($27\frac{1}{2}$ in) at the shoulder and weigh up to 50 kg (110 lb). Obviously a powerful animal, the Akita was once used for deer and bear hunting. Impressed by their size and soundness, American servicemen took them to the United States where they are now becoming established.

Dogs are used in modern warfare for guard and detection work but they have had other army duties in the past. When the Roman legions marched across

Left: The Afghan Hound is one of the most beautiful and spectacular of the Eastern hunting hounds.
Above: Assyrian hunting dogs of the mastiff type were used, amongst other things, for hunting lions. The spiral collars were a device which enabled the hounds to be slipped free quickly when the quarry was sighted.
Right: Milk carts drawn by dogs were a familiar sight on the Continent and in Victorian London. Though they were common in their day, few such carts and harnesses have survived.

Europe, they took part of their food supplies with them in the form of cattle on the hoof. To control and guard these herds went droving dogs: large, sturdy, powerful beasts which, as the beef supply diminished, tended to be left *en route* with the local inhabitants. It is believed that the ancestors of the modern Rottweiler reached Germany in this fashion. When the town of Rottweil became the centre of a cattle area, enough descendants of the Roman dogs were left to form the nucleus of a breed of droving dogs which were used by the cattle merchants. These dogs carried the money for the purchase of the beasts in money bags around their necks and, once the transaction had been made, they herded the newly bought cattle back to town for their masters. During the nineteenth century the movement of large numbers of cattle waned, and so did interest in the dogs that drove them. At this point the Rottweiler might have become extinct, like a number of other breeds whose working function had been superceded by the advance of technology. However, by the beginning of the twentieth century the German police were already starting to interest themselves in training dogs extensively for guard and army work. The Rottweiler joined a handful of other breeds considered suitable for this purpose. By the

mid-1930s there were sufficient of them in the United States for them to be officially recognized by the American Kennel Club. By the 1960s they were firmly established in Britain and many other parts of the world.

Although the newcomer to dogs may feel that there is a bewildering multitude of different breeds, many types have become extinct and some others are so few in numbers that their future seems doubtful. The Old English Mastiff is one breed which has had a rather chequered existence. It is usually considered, with the Bulldog, to be an essentially British dog, but it seems unlikely that the breed originated in the British Isles. The Assyrians took mastiff-like dogs into war with them and it seems possible that these dogs were introduced to Britain by the Phoenecian traders, who sailed their merchant ships from the Mediterranean in the sixth century BC to buy tin from the Cornish mines. By the time the Roman legions arrived in Britain the mastiffs were so ferocious that they impressed the new conquerors sufficiently for numbers to be sent back to Rome to take part in the wild beast fights staged in the Roman arenas.

In the time of the first Queen Elizabeth the Mastiff was still going strong as a bull and bear baiting dog. When these sports were prohibited the Mastiff declined in numbers, but it made a partial recovery early in the present century when there was a revival of interest in distinctive and unusual breeds. However, food scarcity in Britain during the Second World War so decimated the breed's numbers that when peace came there was no longer a viable breeding stock. Fortunately, some Mastiffs had been sent to America, and it was their descendants that British breeders reimported to revive the breed. If a dog so large as the Mastiff is to survive anywhere, its future seems to be more assured in America where there is still space and money for the really big breeds, rather than in its economically straitened homeland.

Dogs have always been valued articles of commerce and trade, and since for so many centuries hunting was a passion among the nobility of most European and Eastern countries, hounds of proven ability were

a favourite diplomatic gift between courts and castles. The geneaology of some of the hounds which hunt by scent is fascinating and spans the Western world.

The greatest number of different types of hound were developed in France, for the French nobility, prior to the Revolution, looked upon hunting as a form of art. One of the greatest, and the earliest, of French hounds was the St Hubert's Hound, named after the Abbey of St Hubert founded in the Ardennes in AD 687. The Church was, in those times, a career rather than a vocation, and the Abbot was able to indulge his passion for hunting. The monks bred two kinds of heavy hunting hounds, one all black and one all white. These dogs were remarkable for their scenting powers and their melodious voices. They became very famous and much sought after.

The modern Bloodhound breed is descended from the black St Hubert Hound, a breed which is also distinguished by its remarkable ability to follow a cool trail long after other trailing hounds have given up. Dogs of the black St Hubert strain, crossed with early American Foxhounds, gave rise to the Cuban Bloodhound, which was used to hunt slaves who tried to escape from the West Indian sugar plantations. From the same sources came the American Coonhound or, to be more exact, the Black and Tan Coonhound. The other five Coonhound breeds tend to have much more foxhound blood and therefore descend more from the other branch of the St Hubert family tree.

When the Norman invaders conquered England in 1066 they looked down with snobbish distaste upon the way in which the natives hunted vermin and imported their own hounds to hunt stag, the only proper quarry for a Norman gentleman. These hounds were the descendants of the white St Hubert's

Hound and were called Talbot Hounds, after a family from the Ardennes which settled in England in the eleventh century. The Talbot was common in the Middle Ages but now is only remembered in the name and signboards of some inns, for it became extinct by the end of the seventeenth century. It had by then given rise to the Southern Hound, which was a heavily built, short-legged hound, still with the excellent scenting powers and melodious voice of its St Hubert ancestor. The Southern Hound had pendulous ears and dewlap but it was a slow worker, so when fox hunting started to become a popular sport, about 1700, the Southern Hound was crossed with more lightly built dogs to give it greater speed, thus producing the first English Foxhounds and Harriers.

American settlers imported packs of hounds in the seventeenth and eighteenth centuries. These packs came from Ireland and France as well as from England, and from them developed the American Foxhound, a leggier, more lightly built hound than its English counterpart. Thus the St Hubert strain, diluted in various ways over the past thousand years, stands behind a number of modern breeds on both sides of the Atlantic.

Dogs associated with the aristocracy tend to fare as badly as their masters in revolutionary times. Many packs of hounds were decimated beyond recovery during the French Revolution. The same fate seems to have befallen the Russian Wolfhound, or Borzoi, in its native land. This fine breed evolved from crossing the Persian Greyhound, which had speed and courage but could not withstand a Russian winter, with a native sheepdog which was also long-legged, but had a thick, wavy coat capable of keeping out the cold. Once the breed type had been established, wolf hunting became an extravagant ritual. The best-documented of these hunts, the Perchino, fielded 60–100 Borzois at a time. The dogs, leashed in pairs that were matched for colour, speed and courage, were held by liveried huntsmen around the perimeter of the area chosen for the hunt. A pack of foxhounds was used to flush out all the game in coverts and the nearest Borzois were slipped as soon as a wolf appeared. The dogs were expected to pin the wolf down until the huntsmen arrived. The wolf was not necessarily killed and in the case of the Perchino hunt was usually pinioned and gagged, then kept to be let loose and coursed on later occasions.

Borzois did not reach the West until two were presented to Queen Victoria by the Czar of Russia. These dogs were received so favourably that the Czar presented more and the English aristocracy took up the breed. The first Borzois to reach America came from England, but these were shortly followed by direct imports from Russia. By the time of the Russian Revolution, enough stock was abroad to ensure the continuance of a breed which the new Russian rulers had no time for, it being a symbol to them of the system they had overthrown and wished to forget.

Opposite: A hound, held on a leash by a huntsman, attempts to find the scent of a stag. When the quarry has been found, the rest of the pack will be unleashed to pursue it. This illustration is from a fourteenth-century book on hunting, but the same methods had been used by the Greeks and Romans.

Right: The Irish Wolfhound is credited with being the tallest breed of dog in the world. Like most of the really large breeds, it is a gentle and affectionate dog. Its distant past, however, was far from peaceful, for dogs of this type accompanied the Celts into battle and were the guards and hunting hounds of the early Irish kings. Though its name indicates that it was used for hunting wolves, it is probable that it was expected to tackle all the larger beasts of prey.

Below: Dogs like these Pharaoh Hounds were known to the ancient Egyptians. They are very active, fast and agile sporting dogs which are used on their native island of Malta for rabbit hunting. The rich tan of their colouring is one of their most attractive features.

Wealthy exiles from their homeland often took with them the dogs that had had a place in their former lives. These were not only sporting and working dogs – pet and toy breeds were always an important feature of life as well. In this way the Pug reached England with the court of William of Orange when he went to England to share the throne with his wife Queen Mary. The Pug had already travelled halfway around the world, for it originated in China where there was an interest in breeding small, short-nosed pet dogs. From China the Pug reached the Dutch East Indies and thence was taken back to Holland, where their curiosity value made them fashionable. They became the rage in England too during the eighteenth century, for no lady of title was considered fully accoutred unless she had a Negro page boy and a Pug dog. In this period the Pug had the whole of its ears cropped off, a barbarous and cruel practice, the pain of which was presumed to deepen the furrows and wrinkles on the dog's forehead. Contemporary pictures, and the many china models of the breed made then, show the dog with these heavily cropped ears and the custom did not die out until the 1800s.

The most famous strain of Pugs in the middle of the nineteenth century was the Willoughby Pug, a silver fawn dog with a distinct dark trace marking down its back. Toy dogs have always been lucrative booty for professional dog thieves and a Willoughby Pug was the subject of one well-documented theft. The thieves had an order for such a dog to be shipped out to America. Only one animal of the required colour was known to be in London and that belonged to an elderly lady whose habit was to walk it down Regent Street every afternoon. While the lady gazed at the goods displayed in the elegant shop windows the

thieves approached, unhooked the Willoughby Pug from its leash and substituted a more ordinary dog of their own without her noticing.

European Pugs became heavier, more cobby dogs than their Chinese forefathers, a point which was emphasized when the first black Pugs appeared in Britain in the 1880s. These dogs had been purchased in China by a Lady Brassey during a voyage on the yacht *Sunbeam*. The black Pugs were not as massive nor as compact as the fawn variety established in Britain, but since then the two types have merged.

It is rather surprising that the Pug should have increased in weight and size since reaching Europe, when for most breeders the desired aim in many toy breeds is to produce them as small as possible. Tradition says that the ladies of ancient Greece, where the little dog we now know as the Maltese was a popular pet, endeavoured to keep their dogs small enough to be carried by dosing the puppies with alcohol and keeping them shut in small dark cages. Similarly the Mexicans are supposed to have administered native gin to the Chihuahua to ensure that it did not grow too big. However, breeding down the size in any type of dog is a considerably more complicated process than that, taking numerous generations to achieve and providing many pitfalls.

One of the most successful examples of the miniaturization of a breed was carried out in the nineteenth century with the Pomeranian. White Pomeranians of about 9 kg (20 lb) weight were one of the most popular pets of the mid-Victorian era. There were few smaller ones and none less than about 3.5 kg (8 lb). Yet within a space of about 25 years breeders produced a perfect toy dog, averaging about 1.8 kg (4 lb) in weight and sometimes as small as 680 g ($1\frac{1}{2}$ lb)

Opposite: This eighteenth-century pair of porcelain pugs is now a collector's item. The heavily cropped ears were fashionable then.
Above: The modern Pug.

fully grown. These dogs came in a variety of shades and retained all the vivacity and activity of their larger relatives whom they completely eclipsed. Nothing but the toy Pomeranian is now ever seen outside Continental Europe and, strangely enough, the white colour, which was once so popular, has fallen completely out of favour.

One group of dogs, the European toy spaniels, might perhaps claim to have the best authenticated of histories, for they have appeared in more portraits from the sixteenth century onwards than any other type of dog. They are represented today by three main breeds: the King Charles, the Cavalier and the Papillon. The toy spaniels gambolling around the feet of their owners in paintings by Titian, Paul Veronese and other old masters were slim in build and had long muzzles and straight, rather than curled, tails. They are smaller versions of the type of spaniel then used for sport. By the nineteenth century, this type of small dog had largely disappeared, having given rise to the Papillon and the King Charles, the latter being evolved by crossing with the Pug to give the domed head and flattened nose. The Cavalier represents a twentieth-century attempt to reproduce the original type. So successful has this been that it is now one of the most popular of modern toy dogs in Britain.

A dog of your own

No one should embark upon the adventure of owning any animal without first finding out as much as possible about it, at the same time taking a careful look at themselves, and then thinking seriously about how well the two of them will suit each other. Giving an animal as a present to someone else demands even greater care and a pet should never be a total surprise, for one must be absolutely certain that the recipient is prepared for the responsibility it entails. Too many people are captivated by bright eyes and a wagging tail but, faced with the demands which a dog will make upon their time, wish that they had realized just what they were letting themselves in for and had not responded quite so impulsively to its appeal. Even worse are those occasions when people, thinking of a pet – quite wrongly – as a plaything, become tired of it and have no conscience about getting rid of it as soon as possible and embarking upon some new foible.

Looking after a dog, whether it is a cheeky mongrel or the aristocratic bearer of a distinguished pedigree, can use up a lot of time, energy and patience, and may prove quite expensive when food, veterinary bills, kennel charges and – for some breeds – clipping costs have been taken into account. Once undertaken, these are responsibilities that you do not have the right to jettison and they will continue for many years. Is the pattern of life you see ahead one which will continue to give you the time you will need for your dog? Who will look after a teenager's devoted companion when its owner grows up and leaves home to go to university or to work and cannot take it too? Could your work take you to live in other countries where quarantine regulations might separate you from your pet? Few of us can plan far into the future but we would do well to remember that a dog will be an added complication – for even in personal relationships it is wise not to forget that old adage

'Love me, love my dog'. Dog ownership should never be entered into lightly or on impulse.

First, seriously consider whether you really want a pet of any kind, with all the responsibilities it will entail; then think whether that pet should be a dog – there are many animals that require much less attention, cost less, or whose briefer lifespans may be more suited to your particular circumstances. As well as needing grooming, food and exercise, dogs are sociable animals and need companionship – if you and your family are away at work all day choose some other pet that is less demanding in this respect. Every dog should be accustomed to being left alone quietly for three or four hours at a time, but to leave an animal for ten hours daily is a thoughtless cruelty.

If you are convinced that dog owning is for you, then you can go on to consider the kind of dog you need. How do you discover which type will suit you best? All puppies tend to be irresistible and, since you cannot have a trial run or trade a puppy in, as you would a car, the decision cannot be made on their immediate appeal. Dogs are adaptable creatures, which is why they are such successful pets, but they have basic needs which must be fulfilled and these vary from breed to breed, so perhaps it would be better to rephrase the question and ask 'Which breed would your way of life suit best?'

There are so many breeds registered with the Kennel Club that the choice seems embarrassingly wide and then there are mongrel dogs in all kinds of permutations. Should you buy a pedigree dog? The initial price will be higher than you will pay for a mongrel, but when you consider how much you will spend on its upkeep during its life the difference may seem insignificant. Some people believe that mongrels are healthier and more intelligent than pure-bred animals, but there is no evidence to support this view. You are just as likely to end up with a moronic mongrel as a stupid thoroughbred. If you are absolutely sure of a mongrel puppy's parentage and know both dogs well you may be able to make a reasonable guess at the kind of adult dog which will result, but in most cases this is very difficult to predict.

Top: Particolour or harlequin poodles like these were often circus and showman's dogs. These cannot be exhibited as only solid colours are allowed in the show ring. **Bottom**: The Tibetan Spaniel is a convenient size and makes a good watchdog.

15

What could provide a greater contrast than the
Afghan Hound at the top and the miniature
Dachshund at the bottom?

Which genes will be dominant? Will you end up with a
miniature or a giant that fills the house? Will the dog
inherit gentle characteristics or is it the offspring of a
particularly savage stray? With the care and attention
that their owners give them, most mongrels grow into
delightful pets, but the advantage of having a pedigree
dog is that its careful breeding means that you can
know for certain what the adult dog will be like. You
know exactly what you are getting in the way of size

and looks and can have a fair idea of the temperament
to expect. Nevertheless the adult dog will develop
according to the way you raise it, becoming very much
what you make it. Your attitude to strangers and to
outside events, your reactions to the puppy and its
behaviour, do a lot to determine whether your dog
will be a well-mannered, well-adjusted individual or a
wild antisocial hooligan.

If you want a dog which can be trained to do a
particular job of work you should choose from the
breeds which have been developed to specialize in that
task, but even the choice of family pet should pay

regard to the background of the various breeds for it has great relevance to the kind of dog they are. Some breeds are familiar to us all – the German Shepherd Dog (also known as the Alsatian), the Poodle and the Labrador, while some seem so rare and exotic as to sound almost unbelievable – the hairless Chinese Crested, for example, or, at the opposite end of the scale, the Hungarian Puli, with so much hair hanging down to the ground in corded strands that it is difficult to tell at first sight whether the dog is coming or going. Indeed, the enormous variety of shapes, sizes, colours and markings make it difficult to believe that all breeds of dog are descended from a common ancestor, and it is fascinating to speculate on where all the differences came from and how each one became established as a characteristic peculiar to a particular breed. However, dog experts are generally agreed that all dogs can be placed in one or other of a number of broad groups. The British and American Kennel Clubs divide breeds into six main groups – although they make their divisions differently – and Continental Clubs usually divide them into seven for show purposes, but both appearance and origin enable us to place any dog into the following broad divisions which were first published by Mr Clifford Hubbard in 1948.

Greyhounds are coursing dogs bred to chase fast-moving prey, following them by sight rather than by scent. They have long legs, tucked-up loins, a pointed muzzle and a streamlined build.

Mastiffs were used to fight in battle in early times and have a long history as guard dogs. They are heavy in both weight and build and have a large, square head.

Sheepdogs are very varied in appearance, often differing very markedly in looks from dogs doing the same job elsewhere for they have been developed very regionally. They have been developed for herding cattle, goats and pigs as well as sheep and have great intelligence, well-developed senses and an untiring gait.

Spaniels, together with the related pointers, retrievers and setters, were all developed as sporting dogs and more particularly in recent centuries as gundogs.

Terriers were developed as vermin hunters and are small to medium size dogs which often still retain the instinct to go to earth after a fox or badger.

Hounds are medium to large in size and are hunting dogs which use the scent of the quarry to keep on its trail.

The appearance of a puppy can be very misleading as to what it will be like as an adult dog so it is essential that you make your choice in terms of the characteristics of the adult of the breed.

Books like this and the many detailed works on individual breeds will give you a good idea of what to expect, but do not make up your mind until you have talked to owners or breeders and seen the breed of your potential choice in the flesh. There may be something which you had not thought of which makes the breed quite wrong for you – for instance, the laboured breathing of the brachycephalic breeds, like Pugs, or the high-pitched bark of some terriers, which some people find very irritating.

Size will be an important consideration, for a big dog will not fit easily into a small flat. If your home is full of precious objects set upon low tables, a strongly swishing tail at just that height could create havoc. If you live in town, with little space available in the vicinity for exercise, then you should also choose a breed that is of the smaller variety. You may fancy the idea of a powerful guard dog such as a Great Dane, a German Shepherd or a Doberman – and large dogs in general seem to be currently fashionable – but unless you can find the space in which to let them gallop about safely off the lead and have the time in which to exercise them, you should confine your ideas to a dog which will more easily fit in with your home and way of life. If you do not want to have hairs all over your carpets and soft furnishings, then look out for a breed that does not shed its coat or at least be prepared for either very frequent grooming or keeping the dog out of a large part of the house. All long-coated breeds are likely to need grooming at least three times a week and bathing several times during the year. Shaggy dogs such as Old English Sheepdogs or Afghans are liable to bring an enormous amount of mud into the house if they are not carefully dried when they come indoors on a wet day.

Some terriers, especially West Highland Whites, Fox Terriers and Jack Russells, have a reputation for being intolerant of children and do not usually make very good family pets. They look so adorable as puppies that many families buy them on the spur of the moment, only to find that the dog's interest lies more in scents and chasing rabbits than in playing games with the family. They are apt to disappear following a trail, to the frustration of the owner whose calls go quite unheeded.

German Shepherd Dogs and Great Danes, on the other hand, can become so utterly devoted to their families that they fret inconsolably if they are left behind when their owners go on holiday, even for a short period. The Cavalier King Charles Spaniel is one breed that, although always ready for a romp or a long walk, does not fret unduly if it has to stay quietly indoors or go into kennels while its owners are away. These little dogs love everybody (whereas some other breeds prove to be a case of 'one man's dog'), their coats need relatively little grooming except for the occasional wash if their 'trousers' become soiled, they are intelligent, clean, cheap to feed and good mixers into the bargain.

Some of the larger breeds, especially those originally bred as guard or fighting dogs, need very firm discipline if they are not to take control. Dogs are pack animals and are led by the dominant animal in the pack – and that instinct is still very much alive. It is important that the owner should be able to control the dog and dominate it. It is the dog's willingness to accept a human master as a substitute for a canine pack leader that makes it easier to train than most other animals, but if the dog is more confident – or more intelligent – than its owner it is likely to become a very difficult and disobedient animal. Big dogs naturally tend to eat much more than little ones and potential owners should be ready for proportionally high food bills.

Miniature, or 'toy' dogs as they are frequently called, cost less to feed than the bigger breeds, they take up less room in a house or vehicle, are easier to take by bus or train (in some countries big dogs are barred from public transport), need far less exercise and usually take less time to groom. But do not expect a pedigree dog of a small breed to cost less than one of the large dogs. In fact they may well prove more expensive, for while a litter of one of the larger breeds may contain ten or even fifteen puppies, the toy breeds will be more likely to produce a maximum of only four and consequently the puppies fetch higher prices.

Experienced breeders and dog owners consider that some breeds make better household pets than others. Opinions will vary and it is worth giving them all a hearing. The famous trainer Barbara Woodhouse made this selection of the breeds which she considered were the best family pets. She has made her selection from the better known breeds and not included any of the more recently registered dogs which may be more difficult to find.

Small Breeds
Poodles, English Toy Terriers, King Charles Spaniels, Cavalier King Charles Spaniels, Boston Terriers, Pugs, French Bulldogs, Griffons, Corgis (if trained early), Dachshunds, spaniels of all types (with the exception of the Red Cocker whose temperament has deteriorated over the years) and Schipperkes. Beagles also make happy, tolerant family dogs, but are not easily trained and are rather too interested in outdoor scents to be ideal family pets.

Medium Breeds
Labradors of the smaller variety (bitches being better than dogs), Golden Retrievers, Weimaraners, German Shepherd Dogs with good temperaments, English Setters and Gordon Setters, Boxers and Bearded Collies (but not Border Collies which are working dogs and not happy as family pets). Basset Hounds are also suitable if you do not mind an indolent, good-natured, rather dim dog as far as obedience training goes. They do not mind children at all, but prefer to keep their noses to the ground when out walking – which can perhaps prove more funny than fun.

Large Breeds
St Bernards, Newfoundlands and Great Danes. It is important that Great Danes have an early training in implicit obedience. They need a lot of rest, vast amounts of calcium and nourishing food with vitamins to keep them healthy during their staggering rate of growth (something which applies to all big

breeds) and no exercise beyond what they wish for the first six months of their lives.

A word of warning to those who are attracted by the beauty and elegance of coursing dogs such as the Afghan, the Borzoi and the Saluki: they have been bred to follow their quarry as soon as they are unleashed and have a very independent spirit. They are not dogs for anyone without a strong personality. For all their grace they are tough hunting dogs and need firm control. They make excellent guard dogs too, but if you cannot provide them with a wide open space to gallop across it would not be fair to keep them – and even then you must have the patience to wait for them to return to you in their own time, for they may well ignore all calls until they are good and ready.

Having decided what breed of dog you want, you must decide whether you want to have a male or a female. This is very much a matter of personal preference, for loyalty, affection, guarding ability and obedience are qualities found in the individual dog rather than in a particular sex. Bitches are usually more easily trained because their concentration is not being constantly distracted by the sexual signals that male animals go sniffing for on every post and tree. However, bitches come into season twice a year and for a period of up to three weeks, when they are sexually attractive to male dogs, they must be kept closely confined if you do not want them to present you with a litter of puppies. Naturally, if you do want to raise puppies you will choose a bitch.

Given the conditions under which most dogs live today a dog's sexuality is rarely of any benefit to either dog or man, for the restraints that people put upon their pets only cause their dogs frustration. Although the sex instinct can be removed by a simple surgical operation it is still comparatively unusual for dog owners to have their pets neutered, although with cats it is becoming an accepted practice. Unless you have a particularly fine pedigree animal, or own a breed which is low in numbers, you should seriously consider having a dog castrated or a bitch spayed. It is true that bitches can be given a contraceptive pill like that taken by many women, but we cannot monitor its action and control any undesirable side-effects as easily as in humans and, unless it is proposed to merely suppress a single heat prior to a later mating, it is much more sensible to operate for good.

The castrated dog is not only a happier dog, free from the worry and frustration of local bitches, it is also a much nicer animal to have around. It will lose some of its pack leader instinct, which will only make it less likely to mark its territory by urinating on your

Top: The Hungarian Puli has a coat hanging in long cords which provides complete protection against the weather. **Bottom:** The Chinese Crested is one of the hairless breeds and needs protection both from sunburn and extreme cold.

furniture, less likely to fight other dogs and more submissive to the wishes of its human pack leader. There is no evidence that it alters any of the other instincts at all, and dogs guard, hunt, work sheep and retrieve game just as well after castration as before.

It is most important that dogs should be castrated after they have reached maturity, otherwise they lack character and initiative and become lazy, fat 'eunuchs'. The age at which a dog reaches sexual maturity varies enormously between individuals. Generally speaking, small breeds mature more quickly than large ones. The first clear indication is when the dog starts 'lifting its leg', which may be as early as six months or as late as eighteen months. It is usually better to castrate too late than too early, and dogs have been castrated at six or seven years old with no ill effects. It is better to leave a submissive dog until it is older, while a dominant one should be operated on much sooner.

Similarly, bitches should not be spayed until they have come in season at least once. Bitches spayed too early tend to be overweight and obese, which affects them mentally just as much as physically. Unlike castration, spaying done at the right time does not change a bitch's character all. Spayed bitches also seem to be healthier, with fewer uterine disorders and no risk of false pregnancies.

In almost every town and city you will find a pet shop where you can buy a puppy and some of them are very good indeed, but they are rarely themselves responsible for the breeding of their dogs and, in consequence, the chances are that the best puppies of a litter have been sold directly by the breeder. In any case, it is most helpful to see a puppy with its mother and litter mates, to know how it has been fed and to discuss the level of development which it has reached. Not many breeders advertise their stock in the daily

press but your newspaper shop will be able to order the dog papers which are published in every country and which do carry breeders' advertisements.

Tell the breeder what you want. If you need a top quality dog with show potential – and are prepared to pay the extra cost – you can discuss the dog's pedigree in detail. (By the way, if you plan to show a dog he should *not* be neutered.) If you want a pet and are more concerned with personality than some minor defect in appearance, you will be offered an equally well-reared dog which will make a fine companion – indeed you might find the blemish in line or marking makes him more attractive than the official standard in your eyes.

Choosing a puppy from a litter is not an easy task – you may find that instead a pup has chosen you and is not to be resisted. If you have any doubt about the breeder's reputation, check that the surroundings are clean and vermin-free. A healthy puppy is plump but should not be unduly pot-bellied. Do not accept a dog that has a discharge coming from its eyes or nose – it may be nothing, but do not take risks. Look for a puppy with loose, supple skin and clear bright eyes, one that is bold and lively and does not hang back or hide in corners. The first to come running to you may perhaps be particularly dominant and would not be the best choice for a very gentle person unless the mother and her strain were known to be particularly gentle dogs. If even one of a litter looks ill do not take any of them, for the infection is likely to have been passed on and you do not want to spend your first weeks with a new dog fighting to keep him alive.

If you can afford to keep more than one dog, consider taking two puppies. They will keep each other company, play together and grow together and you need not feel so conscience-stricken if you have to leave them on their own. However, if they are to be kept as pets you should choose two of the same sex.

Most people automatically buy a puppy when acquiring a dog and take pleasure in moulding the puppy's behaviour to suit their own life style and in watching him develop, but if someone asks you to take an adult dog do not automatically turn him down. It may not be possible to change the training or eradicate the habits he has already developed but he can become attached to you and be as much *your* dog as any puppy, for the loyalty and affection that he shows you will reflect your treatment of him, not the dog's age. Find out why an adult dog is on the market or looking for a home: its owner may have died or had to go abroad and not been able to take him too, and in many cases it is due to housing difficulties and certainly no fault of the dog's. Offer to take the animal on a week's trial, which will enable you to discover whether the dog can settle in with you and whether he has any bad habits that you cannot tolerate. It is not literally true that you 'can't teach an old dog new tricks' but it is much more difficult to cure an old dog of bad habits than to prevent them in a puppy.

Opposite: The French Bulldog is a relatively modern breed, developed less than a hundred years ago. The French authoress, Colette, had one as a constant companion.
Right: Toy spaniels have been favourites for many centuries. These puppies are King Charles Spaniels, so called because King Charles II was very fond of this type of dog.

Left: This self-portrait of William Hogarth shows him with his pet Pug and gives some idea how the breed has changed since the eighteenth century. Hogarth owned at least two pet Pugs in his lifetime, Crab and Trump. Trump lies buried in the garden of his master's house in Chiswick. A china model of one of Hogarth's Pugs was made by the Chelsea potteries in 1760.

Above: Rat-catching contests were a popular betting sport of the eighteenth and nineteenth centuries. Several dogs were backed against each other to see which could kill the most in a set time, or one dog was backed to kill a certain number in so many minutes. Rat pits had smooth, boarded walls with a triangular guard fixed at the top of each corner to prevent the rats from climbing out. The rats huddled in the corners, with the wisest buried deepest and farthest from danger. A good ratting dog wasted no time chasing but picked the rodents off one by one from the outside of the pile. The dog shown here is likely to have been one of the ancestors of the English Toy Terrier.

Left: The Pekinese is one of the most popular toy dogs in the Western world. Many people, who have only owned larger breeds, tend to be scornful of the toys. In fact most are as hardy and intelligent as their larger relatives and make up for their lack of size with an abundance of character and energy.
Above: Three long-coat Chihuahuas and a smooth.

Top left: The Papillon, or Butterfly Dog, is one of the group of European toy spaniels. When adult this puppy will have heavily fringed ears which are meant to resemble the wings of a butterfly, whilst the white blaze down the dog's forehead represents the insect's body. These very vivacious little dogs have distinguished themselves in both beauty and obedience shows.

Bottom left: The Boston Terrier is the national breed of America and a very popular dog in the States. Though this dog has natural ears, they are usually cropped. Brindle and white is the preferred colour, though black and white is permitted. **Right:** The Great Dane is one of the giant breeds and needs an owner with both space and money. The bed this dog is lying on is ideal for so big a breed. The mattress helps to prevent the calouses on elbows and hocks to which the heavyweight breeds are prone.

Above: A well-trimmed Bedlington Terrier has a deceptively lamb-like appearance. The dog has, however, all the courage and fire associated with the terrier breeds, of which it is probably the fastest and most graceful.

Right: The Borzoi, or Russian Wolfhound, has an aristocratic elegance which is an eloquent reminder of its past as a companion and hunting dog of the Russian Czars and nobility.

Above: The Chow is a very old Chinese breed which has been used for a variety of purposes in its native land, including that of guard dog, gundog and draught dog. It has also been bred for both its meat and fur. The two breed characteristics which are peculiar to Chows are the blue-black tongue and the almost straight hind leg which gives them a stilted gait. They are very loyal to their owners but have little interest in anyone else.

Right: A late eighteenth-century portrait by Louis Leopold Boilly of a toy spaniel shows that these little dogs were really smaller versions of the sporting spaniels in use as gundogs. The charm of these miniatures is well shown in this portrait and it is easy to see how their popularity was so widespread for such a long period of time.

Taking care of your dog

Taking care of a new dog begins when you decide that you are going to have him (or her). You need to prepare by getting a box or basket for him to sleep in, food and water bowls, a brush for grooming, a comb, nail clippers, a collar and lead. If he is a puppy, arrange newspaper in the area you plan to be his and, if possible, surround it with a children's wire playpen so that he cannot wander into danger. You can buy or make a few toys and you should certainly have a box or basket to carry him in, or a rug to wrap him up in, on the journey from the breeder. A towel and a small bowl may be useful too in case his first journey should make him travel sick – the towel is to spread across your lap.

It is not only the basic equipment that has to be provided, you must plan the puppy's arrival so that it will be a quiet time when you can be with him and there will not be crowds of people or boisterous children about to frighten him.

A small wooden box, turned upon its side and with a batten nailed across the bottom to stop his blanket or cushion from falling out, will suit a puppy of one of the small breeds better than a basket. It plays a double role in that by turning it with the opening at the top he will not be able to climb out and can be accustomed to being left at home alone. Some people recommend that a hot water bottle wrapped in a piece of cloth or blanket will console him for the loss of his litter mates, but do not leave it to go cold. For the first few nights you will probably find that he will howl at being left when everyone goes to bed. You must just be tough and put the pillow over your ears for if you start by giving way, however plaintively he may call, you will find that you are rearing a dog that is always pestering you and expects you to wait upon him rather than learning to obey you.

Left: The Saluki is one of the greyhound group and amongst the oldest of the world's hunting hounds. They were kept by the nomadic Bedouin to hunt gazelle and desert hare and did not become known to the Western world until the twentieth century.

Before you leave the breeder's make sure that you have the dog's pedigree, find out whether it has had any vaccinations and ask for the certificates showing which have been given. Discover exactly what he has been eating – many breeders will provide a diet sheet – and follow the same regimen, gradually introducing changes if you prefer to offer different food. Find out when and how often meals have been given: at six weeks a puppy should be having four meals a day, but at about four months this can be cut down to three, and by six months to only two and eventually, if you wish, to a single daily meal when he is about 12 months old. Naturally the amount of food he needs will increase as he gets older.

The most important thing to remember with a young puppy is that he is still a baby. Many new owners make the mistake of starting to house train a puppy the moment they get him home without thinking what they are doing. They take this infant from his brothers and sisters and familiar surroundings, probably subject him to a long journey in a strange box on wheels, then put him down in the middle of a strange kitchen floor. Nervous, and with a bursting bladder after such a journey, he immediately does what any sensible person would expect him to do but the owner then smacks him for making a puddle on the floor. Animals do not reason out the whys and wherefores, they learn by association, and the chances are that the puppy will associate the smack with the owner rather than with the puddle, making him feel immediately insecure. Such treatment turns many confident, friendly puppies into nervous, timid creatures within days of them arriving in a new home. It is amazing the way in which parents will wrap their own offspring up in nappies for month after month yet expect a baby dog to go all night without having to relieve himself. It is much wiser to anticipate the inevitable. As soon as you get home gently carry the puppy to wherever you want him to perform his toilet – whether out of doors or on newspaper in the house – and when he has finished praise him for being a good dog. Puppies nearly always want to relieve themselves when they wake up and after they have had a meal. So take yours

out at these times, whether or not it shows any desire to do so. A puppy which has been brought up under clean conditions will soon go towards the door when it feels uncomfortable. All you have to do then is to open the door. But remember that the puppy cannot open the door itself, and he cannot wait until you come back from shopping or finish a long telephone conversation. To punish a puppy which makes a mistake under these circumstances is pointless and cruel.

Few people, however, have the time to keep a constant eye on a puppy. The answer to this is a playpen, very similar to a child's playpen, an essential piece of equipment for the average puppy owner. The pen should be placed as near as possible to the door, with a bed in one corner, and the floor should be covered with newspaper. When you are too busy to keep an eye on the puppy, all you have to do is pop him in his pen. There might appear to be a disadvantage in that the puppy will get into the habit of using the newspaper in the pen and will not want to go outside. But when the puppy is outside the pen, he will tend to go towards the pen if he wants to relieve himself. This should be fairly obvious and you can easily put him outside – hence the reason for the pen being near the door. When eventually you remove the playpen and the newspaper altogether, the puppy will

still head for the same spot and you can then open the door so that he can go outside.

From the beginning you should start to call a dog by his name: and you should choose a name which he can easily recognize when he is called and not confuse with any instruction you may give him. Remember not to use a puppy's name when you are telling him he has been naughty, for if you associate the name with punishment and misdemeanour you may find that he doesn't come when called. A dog should learn to associate his name with pleasure.

If a young dog does occasionally make a puddle, do not punish him – simply pick him up and take him to the right place. He is probably as disturbed about it as you.

The earlier a puppy is introduced to the outside world the easier it will be for him to accept it, for very young puppies are less likely to fear strange people and noises than are older ones – and they are less likely to be carsick. However do not take unnecessary risks. You can take a puppy out for a drive when he is

Above: Children derive a great deal of pleasure from the companionship of puppies but their play needs supervision lest one bully the other.
Right: The Boxer puppies above will grow up to the size shown here. The smaller dog is a Boston Terrier.

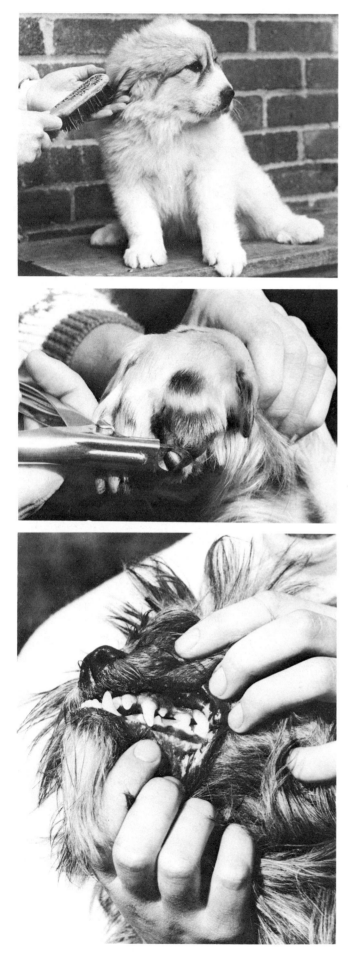

about six weeks old, but if he has not had his inoculations take care not to put him on ground where other dogs may have been for there is a risk of him picking up infections. It is good for a puppy to get used to people and to being handled and fussed over, but keep him away from people who have dogs of their own or handle other dogs – and of course from the dogs themselves. If you take care the risk of picking up an infection will be much less than the risk of the puppy becoming shy of traffic and of people if kept away from them for too long.

Once your puppy is old enough to be inoculated (8–12 weeks), you should consult a veterinary surgeon as there are various types of inoculation. Two inoculations are normally given, which will protect your puppy against distemper, hardpad, hepatitis and two forms of leptospirosis. Booster doses will be necessary at intervals throughout the dog's life.

Remember that it is not a good idea to take an uninoculated puppy into a waiting room with other dogs which may be infected; if possible, try to find a vet with an appointment system so that you can be seen immediately, or wait outside in your car.

Travel sickness can be a problem. Take the puppy out as young as possible, as frequently as possible and for short distances – but never just after a meal! Some dogs are never travel sick but if yours is try to get him over the problem as quickly as possible. There are tranquillizers available which will help. Your veterinary surgeon will advise on the correct drug and dosage for your particular puppy. But do not regard drugs as a cure, only as an aid to help the puppy. Always give the minimum dose, and if it does not work, you can give a little more next time. Reduce the dose as soon as possible until you find that the puppy is happy without being given anything. You can also help your puppy to overcome car sickness by trying to persuade him to associate the car with pleasure. A puppy's first car ride usually takes it away from familiar surroundings to a new home, which he inevitably finds very bewildering. And all too often the next trip is to the vet, who sticks a needle in it. So make a regular car journey, such as driving the children to school, take the puppy with you and feed him when you get home. The children should prevent him thinking too much about himself on the way there, the journey back will be short and he will have his breakfast as a reward. It is also worth taking the

Top: Start gentle grooming as soon as you get your puppy. In this way it will become accustomed to the whole process. Middle: Nail-cutting can be an extremely painful process for a dog, so only take off a little at a time. Bottom: If you look at your dog's teeth regularly it will be that much easier should any treatment ever become necessary. Opposite: Never poke anything down the ear canal as it is possible to injure the ear drum. Clean the flap only and dry thoroughly.

puppy out in the car before giving it a walk. If you take him even a short way in the car and then let him have a romp which he enjoys, he should very soon associate the car with pleasure and be anxious to go in it. When you do have to go on a longer journey, it is often a good idea to stop after the first half hour or so and let the puppy have a run.

Many dogs learn to wait quite patiently in a car while you go shopping, or make a visit where they will not be welcome, but do not leave them there unnecessarily and *never* shut a dog in a closed car or any other confined spaces without making sure that there is adequate ventilation. On a hot day the body temperature may rise rapidly, causing the dog to collapse from heat stroke. Should you ever be in a situation where this happens the simplest treatment is to soak the dog in cold water until he recovers.

Mutual grooming is one of the ways in which wild animals show affection and most dogs will enjoy their grooming sessions, particularly if you get into a regular habit when they are young. Make this an opportunity to check up on overall condition, not just an occasion for a brushing, and make a note of any changes in condition or development. Every pet owner should keep a record card for each of his animals, showing date of birth, when inoculations were given, medical history, when on heat, injuries, etc – it is amazing how difficult it is to remember these things or when a symptom first began to show itself if you do not keep a written record, and such information can be invaluable to your vet if accurately noted down.

It is best to give a dog a few minutes grooming every day and a thorough grooming once a week. You will find it easier to put a small dog on a table and spread out plenty of newspaper to catch hair and dirt. Start your inspection with the head, open the mouth and check the teeth and gums. If the teeth show signs of tartar deposit, you can remove it yourself with a tooth scaler. The teeth must be scaled from the gums to the tip of the tooth. This is fairly simple to do if there is only a light deposit of tartar, but if possible get your veterinary surgeon to show you how to do it correctly before making your first attempt. Heavy tartar causes receding gums, bad breath and decaying teeth. If the teeth have become heavily encrusted consult your vet. As part of the weekly grooming clean the teeth with an ordinary toothbrush which helps to keep the deposits down.

Next check the eyes. These should be bright and clear, and any discharge should be checked with your vet. Some breeds with protruding eyes or very deep-set ones accumulate dirt and dust in the corners, causing irritation and often making the eyes water. One of the best and cheapest eye washes is an ordinary saline solution made by mixing 1 teaspoonful of salt into $\frac{1}{2}$ litre (1 pint) of boiled water and allowing it to cool.

Now check the ears. Spaniels, poodles and other dogs with long, hairy ears pick up all sorts of things on their ear flaps which can mat the hair and cause

discomfort. If the inside of the ear flap is grubby wipe it round with damp cottonwool. Never poke or probe into the ear itself; you cannot see down the ear without a proper instrument and if there is any obstruction you could easily push it down even further. If there is no discharge and the ear smells fresh but it seems to irritate the dog, try pouring a little warm olive oil down it. This should soothe the ear and will help to float out any dirt inside. This simple treatment apart, never mess about with ear troubles but take the dog to the vet.

In very cold or very dry weather some dogs get cracked skin on their noses. Rubbing on a little oil will usually relieve this trouble.

Take a good look at the dog's feet and make sure there are not cuts, thorns in the pads, cysts between the toes or mats of hair. City dogs sometimes get cracked pads from too much walking on hard streets. Again a little oil will often help and the dog can wear special boots for a few days until the pads heal. If there are mats of hair under the pads or between the toes, cut these out very carefully with a pair of sharp, blunt-ended, curved scissors. If these mats are left, they accumulate dirt and set up an irritation which can lead to eczema. This will need professional treatment.

Use a nail clipper and file to keep the dog's nails in trim. The nails have a sensitive 'quick' running down the centre; in a white nail this shows up as a pink streak. Care should be taken to avoid cutting this, as not only is it painful for the dog, it also bleeds profusely. If you just cut the pointed tip of the nail, it should be safe even if the dog has black nails where you cannot see the tip. After you have clipped the nails, finish them off with a coarse file, drawing down from the root of the nail to the tip. If you file the nails regularly, the quick recedes and you will not need to use the clippers so frequently.

Keep the nails short and do not forget the dew claws. These are small extra claws found on the inside of the feet, rather like a thumb in humans. They are usually in the forefeet only, but some breeds also have hind

dew claws. As these claws do not reach the ground, they are not worn down and will need regular clipping. If not attended to frequently, they can grow right round into the foot and cause a nasty abscess. In some breeds dew claws are removed.

Under the dog's tail are two small glands set on each side of the anus. An evil smelling liquid collects in them which can cause an abscess if it is not removed. The wild dog's diet includes skin and bones and they help to keep the anal glands emptied but the domestic dog usually has less roughage to eat and needs your help. It is a simple job when you know how: just hold a pad of cottonwool over the glands and squeeze firmly on either side – ask your vet to show you how.

It does not take much effort to keep a short-coated dog in clean condition but short-coated dogs do tend to shed their coat a lot. This is partly because most dogs live in centrally heated houses and spend much of their time in artificial light which conflicts with the body's response to the seasons which make it shed naturally. Usually a good brushing with a stiff bristled brush, hound glove or mitt and a final polish with your hands should be enough. A rubber hound glove will help remove the dead coat.

Long-coated breeds demand a different technique. You need a good stiff brush with longer bristles and a comb with wide teeth. The comb should be used as little as possible so that the coat is not pulled out unnecessarily. Start at the rear end and vigorously brush out the coat, a little at a time until you reach the head. Then go back over the whole dog again. Comb out the feathering on the ears, tail and legs, but do it very carefully. Tease out any small mats of hair with your fingers.

Terriers need special treatment. Unless they are of the smooth variety, such as the Smooth Fox Terrier, they will require regular 'stripping'. Terriers should have a soft thick undercoat and a harsh top coat. When the dog needs stripping the outer, hard coat is pulled out with a stripping knife. This is usually a sort of pen-knife with serrated edges, but there are a number of different types. All terriers are stripped to a different pattern, according to their breed. It is not that difficult to do it yourself, but try to get a breeder to show you how. For daily grooming, the terrier just needs the usual check-over and a good brushing with a stiff brush.

Dogs with thick, stand-off coats like Pomeranians, Keeshonds and Samoyeds need to have their coats brushed up the wrong way first and then carefully brushed back into place. Poodles, which incidentally do not shed their coats like other breeds, need to be

clipped. If you want some of the fancy clips you will need to take the dog to a beauty parlour, but for a simple lamb clip you can learn to do it yourself. You will need either electric or hand clippers and a pair of sharp hairdressing scissors. If you cannot watch someone else to pick up the technique there are a number of specialist books available which will show you how to do the job.

How often your dog will need a bath depends upon the weather and on how dirty he gets. Stand the dog in a sink, bowl or bath of warm water big enough to match his size, pour on shampoo and work up a good lather. Leave the dog's head until last for once it is wet the dog will try to shake. Give the rest of the dog a good washing, and rinse it very well – at least twice in tepid water. Finally wash the head, being careful not to get shampoo into the eyes or to get the inside of the ears wet. If you are outdoors, let the dog out, on a leash, and once it has given a good shake rub it dry with a large rough towel. Indoors, it is best if you put the towel right over the dog to remove the surplus moisture. In either case, an electric hairdryer is ideal for drying the dog off completely, especially for long-haired breeds. At first it may be a little frightening to the dog so get him used to the noise and then, gradually, to the blowing. Brush and comb the coat as you dry it, otherwise it will dry into a tangled mass.

All dogs need exercise – and usually far more than they are given. Left to their own devices they will probably take little, so it is up to you to see they get it: at least thirty minutes free-running exercise each day and more if possible. It will help to keep you fit too. Small dogs can get quite a lot of exercise in a small space but they will appreciate a romp in the open and bigger dogs have to have it. Some of the larger, active breeds, such as Dobermans and German Shepherds, enjoy running beside a bicycle, but do not overdo it or go too fast – and never let a dog run beside a bicycle where there is traffic. Games – especially retrieving – will give the dog more exercise without wearing out your legs and swimming is good for them too.

You will probably find other activities for your dog to enjoy and the more varied exercise you can give him, the more he will benefit. On cold, wet days even small dogs will be all right if kept moving, but don't leave them to stand about doing nothing, and always dry a wet dog on return to the house. In very hot weather, exercise, except swimming, should be carried out in early morning or late evening when it is coolest, as dogs can suffer quite badly from heat stroke.

The dietary needs of an adult dog will vary considerably according to his size and build. A certain amount of food is needed to maintain the normal metabolic processes, and extra is required for activity beyond this, so quantity must be related to the dog's way of life. A working sheepdog, for example, needs much more food than a dog of equal size living in town. A large dog, such as a German Shepherd, needs about 1 kg (2 lb) of meat each day, whereas for a small

dog like a Fox Terrier about 170–225 g (6–8 oz) will suffice. The best way to judge an individual dog's needs is to observe its weight. If he is fat, reduce the intake; if thin, increase it. Appetite is a poor guide since dogs in the wild will immediately eat whatever they can obtain, in case they lack food the next day. By instinct the modern dog still tends to eat all that is put in front of him. The result is the only too common overweight problem seen in household dogs. The diet should include protein in the form of lean fresh meat, carbohydrates such as bread or cereal and fat, which may be dripping, lard, margarine, butter or any vegetable oil. There should be twice as much protein as carbohydrates and about one tenth of the total weight should be fat, remembering that even lean meat contains a little fat.

Loss of condition, a coat that stands on end, loss of weight, dull eyes, lethargy and even too much weight may indicate an incomplete diet or a lack of balance on which you should seek veterinary advice.

Naturally there are times when a special diet is necessary. If your dog has been ill your veterinarian will probably recommend a special high protein diet, and conditions such as nephritis and diabetes will make their own demands, but the most frequent alteration to diet is for the pregnant bitch (see next chapter).

Your own knowledge of your dog will soon become your best guide to its health. If he seems out of sorts do not hesitate to contact your vet, who would rather see you unnecessarily than risk being brought a sick animal which could have been treated earlier. A day off food or a little diarrhoea probably only mean a minor tummy upset but if these symptoms persist they could be the signs of something more serious.

Left: Most dogs, like most humans, do not get enough exercise. By teaching your dog to play games, to catch, to fetch and to jump, you will be rewarded with a happier, healthier animal.
Above: In general the more racily built the breed the more exercise it will need; a Saluki like this needs freedom to gallop in safety. Incidentally this dog is probably travelling at about 50 k/h (32 mph).

Excessive thirst, excessive scratching, holding the head to one side and dull eyes instead of bright ones are all obvious signs that something is wrong and, contrary to popular belief, a cold nose is not always an indication of good health. Severe vomiting which persists demands an immediate visit to the vet.

A distended stomach in a puppy is usually a sign of worms. Most puppies have them, so do not be alarmed and they are easily dealt with in puppies or dogs. You may see them wriggling in the dog's faeces. There are a large number of preparatory worming pills but to be sure that you give the right pill for the type of worm, and in the right dose for your dog, take a small sample of the faeces to the vet. It may not contain any worms but if the dog is carrying these parasites their eggs will almost certainly be there and your vet can discover them by simple tests.

Even more familiar parasites are fleas. The small, red-brown, hard-coated dog flea moves extremely quickly, is hard to catch and difficult to see when on the dog. Small black specks on the skin and sores from scratching are signs of its presence. Occasionally dogs develop an allergy to fleas and break out in lumps and sores over the body, although only one or two fleas may be present. The most effective way of eliminating fleas is to use a flea bath regularly or to follow a control routine available from your vet.

Other external parasites are lice and ticks. Lice are seen as white specks in the hair, usually in clusters and moving slowly. Closer examination shows they have a light orange colour. They are very irritating, causing distress and violent scratching, but can be killed by common parasiticidal baths. In summer ticks may be picked up from long grass. They look like small black peas attached to the skin. Do not pull them out but apply methylated spirit to kill them, then they can be picked off with ease. If they cause abscesses call the vet.

Mange is a skin condition produced by various mites which infest the skin, causing irritation. They spread slowly over the dog causing a very severe condition that may result in death. Mange is contagious to humans so at the first sign of a diffuse, scaly skin condition coupled with hair loss you should see the vet.

Ear mites are similar to the mange mite and may first be indicated by the dog constantly scratching his ears, and confirmed by an inflamed-looking ear with a dark brown wax inside it. Untreated it can result in deformed ears and possibly in loss of balance.

Like you your dog cannot stay young for ever and as he gets old he will not be so active and may develop muscular weakness. Eyes and hearing will not be so good and he probably will not be able to wait so long before being let out to do his toilet. Dogs, like humans, live much longer these days – the oldest recorded died age 27 – but an elderly dog needs consideration and should be given a careful medical check-up every six months.

Rearing a puppy

Raising a litter of puppies can be a fascinating and very satisfying experience but it is not one to be undertaken unless you are prepared to devote plenty of time to giving the mother any help that may be necessary, and are either ready to give the whole litter a home or are quite sure that there are others eagerly waiting to become their owners. Veterinary surgeons are asked to put down so many abandoned or no longer wanted dogs that it would be cruel and unthinking to increase their number. It is true that some puppies fetch very high prices but the expenses that are involved, and the attention that is required, soon disillusion anyone who thinks that dog breeding can be a way of getting rich. Only a large-scale professional breeder is likely to show a profit!

Wild members of the canine family accept whelping and rearing puppies as part of their normal pattern of existence but, as with humans, the more sophisticated and removed from natural conditions they become the greater the need for care and the risk of complications. Some of the very inbred toy and miniature breeds do not seem to have the strength for a normal delivery and frequently require a caesarean section to have their puppies, while breeds such as the Boston Bull Terrier, the Pekingese and the English Bull Terrier, with heavy shoulders and narrow hips, often produce puppies whose foreparts are wider than the mother's pelvic passage. A small bitch mated to a very large dog may also lead to difficulty due to the size of the puppies and naturally any sick dog, or one which has previously suffered a pelvic injury, requires special care.

A female dog usually reaches sexual maturity and first comes into season, or on heat, at about eight to nine months of age, although Chows, for instance, may have their first heat at only five or six months and some dogs not until they are a year or even older. However, any female that shows no sign of heat by 14 or 15 months should be checked out with the vet. The first indication that she is coming into season will usually be a swelling of the vulva, with a discharge from the external genitalia which is at first colourless but after a few days becomes pinkish and bloodstained. This is a perfectly natural preparation for mating in a mammal and no cause for alarm. The coloured discharge usually lasts until about the middle of her season and then reverts to a colourless mucous once again. In most bitches this occurs twice a year but in some it happens only once a year. If you do not want your dog to have puppies, she should be kept in the house or garden where there is no chance of her meeting a male dog and it is advisable to make use of one of the preparations sold to disguise the scent message which the female gives off at this time to signal her condition to male dogs. If you should fail in your vigilance and know that by accident she has mated with a dog whose puppies you do not want her to bear, it is possible to counter conception by administering a drug within 48 hours but, although this will not affect future litters, it is dangerous if given repeatedly.

If you are planning a litter, you will obviously make a very careful selection of the dog you choose to be the father. It is not usual to mate in the first season, and in the case of a very young and inexperienced bitch it is better to choose an older and experienced dog. You should select both for temperament and to maintain and develop the quality of the breed. A bitch is usually ready to be mated when the colour of her discharge begins to disappear, which may be from the seventh to the thirteenth day of heat. One check is to stroke the root of her tail which will make her move her tail from one side to the other if she is ready.

It is usual to take the bitch to the stud dog (whose owner will charge a fee). Both animals should be exercised before they meet and it is a good idea not to feed either for about two hours beforehand. A calm and gentle bitch will cause no problems but one which

Top: A Dandie Dinmont dog gives a cautious sniff at his offspring. The two shades of coat are seen very clearly in the puppies but, as with most breeds, the adult coat colour will be lighter. **Bottom:** This Golden Retriever bitch has every right to look proud of her family. The solid, well-rounded look of these puppies shows that they have been well reared.

is shy, or resents being mated, may turn on the dog and to prevent this happening a bandage should be wound around her muzzle. If she is a maiden bitch it is advisable to consult your vet beforehand or, if you are taking her to an experienced stud owner, to warn him so that he can give any assistance the dogs may require.

Do not insist on being present at the mating. Having seen the stud dog, make yourself scarce once the dogs have been introduced, and ask the owner if you may see the 'tie'. This will be suggested, as being more satisfactory to you both. The bitch will be better without your presence and so will the stud dog and his owner. A troublesome bitch is always better without her owner. Let her rest a bit before the return journey and keep her quiet for a few days after the mating, without violent exercise.

Your bitch should finish her season about three weeks from its start. Her being mated makes no difference to the length of it. The fact that she may go on showing the coloured discharge for some time after the mating is no indication of her having 'missed', as is sometimes thought. It is however noticeable that a bitch in whelp never quite dries up completely. She remains slightly moist and wet during her nine weeks of pregnancy.

It is usually three or four weeks before you will know whether your dog has conceived, or is 'in whelp', as the dog experts call it. At that age your vet will be able to feel the developing embryos. During the period when you cannot be certain many people recommend the addition of wheat germ to the bitch's diet. This provides a source of vitamin E which stimulates the reproductive organs. It should be given in strict accordance with your veterinarian's instructions, or according to the directions on the packet if you purchase it yourself. She should be fed her normal diet for the earlier part of her pregnancy and will not require any additions or supplements, unless your vet recommends them, provided that it includes at least 225 g ($\frac{1}{2}$ lb) of meat each day. She should have plenty of exercise but must not be subjected to undue strain. Ensure, for instance, that she does not run up and down stairs after the third week from mating. This has been known to cause the death of some, if not all, of a litter of puppies. Check that she is not troubled by parasites. Give her a good dusting with an insect powder to clear up any lice or fleas but, unless she is used to frequent baths, do not risk doing this after about the fifth or sixth week. In fact avoid any unusual activity. If she is used to riding in your car by all means take her out with you, but not if it has been a rare event for her. Neither the strain nor the excitement of a novel experience will be good for her while she is carrying her puppies. It is not a good idea, and may be dangerous, to treat a pregnant bitch for worms. This should be done two to four weeks before she comes in season, which can be predicted in the older animal.

Most bitches give birth 60–63 days after mating, many actually on the sixtieth day. From about the fifth week the mother-to-be will require two meals a day – quantities will naturally depend upon the breed and size of the dog and her usual diet and upon the number of puppies she is carrying. Extras should include cod-liver oil, raw egg yolk and bone meal. Milk will also provide a valuable extra source of calcium for bone building. A bitch carrying a large litter will not only need a considerable increase in the amount of food in the latter weeks of pregnancy but she will need to be fed more often, for the pressure of the puppies on her internal organs will make it uncomfortable for her to eat much at one time. The pregnant animal should always be handled and lifted carefully (place one hand under her chest and the other beneath the hind legs to keep her in a horizontal position). After about the fiftieth day get the vet to check that all is well and make plans if there is any indication of difficulty occuring when whelping time arrives. At the last week cut away the hair from around her teats and wash them well. Also trim her hind feathering with trimming scissors (this will save you cutting this away, which might affect her looks) and wash this and her hindquarters well. Repeat the process on the fifty-eighth and fifty-ninth days.

Some bitches do whelp before the sixtieth day but puppies which arrive earlier than the fifty-eighth should be considered premature and will require constant and careful attention. If you think your dog is ready to whelp her temperature will be a fairly reliable guide. If it is normal she is deceiving you, for 12 – sometimes as long as 48 hours – before whelping it will drop by two or three degrees to below 38°C (100°F). If her temperature has *not* dropped there is no need to sit up with her all night.

Where the maternity ward is to be must be decided early in the bitch's pregnancy and she must get used to it some time before she whelps. Her quarters must have some sort of heating, for newly born puppies must be kept warm. More litters are lost through the lack of warmth than from anything else. If they are to be kept in a kennel, run an electric cable out to it and install an infrared lamp to throw heat down onto the box. There is also what is called a 'dull emitter', which is good for heating a kennel in winter, but it is general heating, and not directed downwards, which is the point of the infrared lamp. This keeps the bed warm and dry, and also dries the puppies as they arrive. It should be hung about three feet from the floor of the box, but can be altered according to the behaviour of the bitch. Should you decide to have her indoors, which is best, choose a place where she will be

Top: Sussex Spaniels like these are very low in numbers. Where there is no possibility of outcrossing, infertility can become a problem, making the outlook for breeds like this rather grim. **Bottom**: These Finnish Spitz puppies have all the appeal of cuddly soft toys.

Above: Puppies as young as this are both blind and deaf. The eyes will not open until the tenth to fourteenth day and hearing develops even more slowly. Bitches normally carry their puppies in this fashion if the need arises.
Right: The Sealyham Terrier is a breed with plenty of guts and rather a comic character. Harsh, wiry, white coats like these are easy to keep clean and the breed is a convenient size for both town and country life. The two puppies here are just about the age to be looking for new owners.

undisturbed and not have her nerves continually on edge with people coming in and out.

The bed in which the bitch is to have her puppies should be made up from a box with high sides and back, the top of which can be covered over with a lid or blanket. It must be large enough for her to be able to turn around in comfortably and it is a sensible precaution to fit a rail or shelf 50–75 mm (2–3 in) from the sides and a short way from the floor – distance depending upon breed – which will prevent her pressing against the side and perhaps crushing one of her puppies by accident. Until she is within a day or two of whelping her usual bedding can be used in the box but, as the time approaches, it should be replaced by a lining of newspaper torn into pieces about 150 mm (6 in) square. This can easily be replaced as it becomes soiled and a thick layer of paper will provide a clean bed which the bitch will enjoy tearing up. The puppies cannot get lost under it, as they might if the bed was covered with straw or a blanket.

If your vet is expecting any problems he will have given you specific instructions or arranged to supervise the whelping himself, but even if no complications are expected – and in most cases they are unlikely to occur – you should be ready to give your dog any assistance that may be necessary and to that end you should prepare the following equipment: a thermometer; absorbent wool (cotton wool); a weak solution of permanganate of potash; a small cardboard box, large enough to take a hot-water bottle wrapped in a piece of blanket; two or three small towels; vaseline.

Whelping is a wonderful and thrilling experience in which to assist but if it is the first time you are present at a birth it may seem a little alarming. Remember that it happens innumerable times every day in mammals – including humans – all over the world. It helps to understand precisely what is happening. In most cases a bitch will know exactly what to do and if you just sit by her she will be grateful for your presence. On no account give her any food, either just before or during her whelping, unless it is very protracted, when a small drink of warm milk can be given. This is because you do not want to overload the bladder, which then presses against the uterus, and can hold up the birth of the puppies. Do not interfere with her when she starts scratching up the papers, and throwing them all over the place. This is natural,

showing her instinct to make a comfortable nest.

Actual labour begins with the bitch straining, which becomes more and more frequent until the water bag appears. Usually the bitch breaks the bag by vigorous licking and then licks up the sudden flow of water that results. Shortly after this the first puppy should arrive.

Sometimes the sight of the first puppy upsets a bitch, and she will refuse to have anything to do with it. Then you must quickly free the puppy's head from the bag in which each puppy is born. This membrane is so clear and transparent that at first glance you might not notice it covering the puppy, but once a puppy is born he or she may suffocate if not freed quickly. If the afterbirth is still attached to the puppy sever it with blunt scissors about 25 mm (1 in) away from the body and then briskly rub the puppy with a warm towel to start him breathing. On hearing his voice the bitch will probably get agitated, so quickly put him back with her and encourage her to lick him and stimulate him into life. Until the second puppy arrives, which is generally fairly quickly, she may still not give proper attention to the first but, as the new arrivals appear, she will settle down to the job.

If there is any undue delay between the puppies, and the bitch strains a great deal to no result, it is advisable to call in the vet for there may be something wrong. On the other hand, if she is just sleeping between having puppies and is not distressed, leave her alone and let her rest. Should she rest too long, say more than two or three hours, it is as well to get her up

and perhaps take her out on the lead for a moment. This will start things going again.

In the case of a large litter, the early arrivals can be moved to the warmth of another box with a hotwater bottle, to be thoroughly dried off under the blanket. Remove each one whilst she is busy with the next, and replace them also when she is too occupied to notice.

Each puppy will have an afterbirth attached, which it is normal for the mother to eat when detaching the puppy from the navel cord. Sometimes it comes with the puppy and sometimes after. It is most important that you should know that one has been passed for each puppy. One left behind can cause septicaemia or blood-poisoning, resulting in the death of the bitch. If you have any doubts ring your vet and tell him, as it must be dealt with at once. The womb contracts anything from 20–24 hours after the whelping, so quick action is obviously necessary.

The completion of the whelping can generally be told by the relaxed and peaceful condition of the bitch, who will stretch herself out and give a big sigh, as much as to say 'Well, that's that!' At this stage you should quietly remove all the soiled pieces of paper that remain. Replace them with dry ones, and continue with the paper for the next three days. Then if she is quite peaceful and quiet with the puppies, give her a blanket.

When you feel that the last puppy has arrived and the bitch has settled, offer her a bowl with about $\frac{1}{4}$ litre ($\frac{1}{2}$ pt) warm milk, boiled and thickened with a

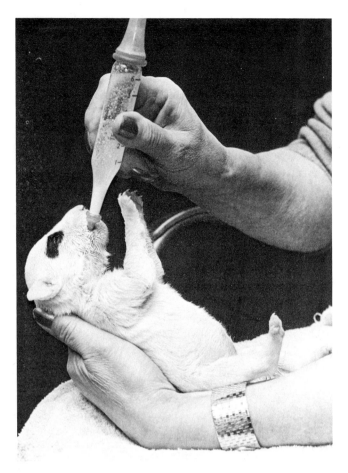

against the practice). This should be done by a professional when the puppy is four days old. In most breeds it is usual to remove the dew claws (although for some the standards require that either front or all dew claws should remain). They can be cut off with sharp scissors. Bleeding can be quickly stopped by dabbing the wound with permanganate of potash solution. Naturally the mother should be removed out of earshot while these operations are carried out, but she can return five or ten minutes later.

While the bitch is nursing her puppies, see they do not make her sore with their sharp little nails. If they do, snip a little off the ends with a pair of curved nail scissors.

From within 24 hours of birth to approximately six weeks old the young puppy suckles milk from its mother, although from four weeks most puppies can successfully be given milk or milk substitutes, with some solid food to lap up. Commercial baby foods are useful here, or milk mixed with finely chopped meat such as chicken or fish. At six weeks the pup should be feeding itself on four meals daily, but do not give biscuit meal before the age of seven weeks. A normal programme would be a morning feed of cereals and milk, shredded or well chopped meat (cooked or raw) at midday and early evening, followed by a late evening meal of milk. Vitamin and calcium supplements may be added to the food.

It is important not to allow any puppy to overfeed and become fat, especially the big breeds, for their legs can easily be made crooked if their bodies become too heavy before the bone has hardened.

The big hounds and guard dog breeds grow very quickly, so it is most essential you do not forget their vitamins and calcium. If by any chance one does seem to be getting too fat, cut down on his biscuit meal and bread rather than on his meat or milk.

On no account let any puppy rush madly about immediately after feeding; certainly put him out to relieve himself but let him rest after food. All puppies need plenty of sleep and they should have a special pen where they can be left in peace, not only to digest their food but to grow too. Put several layers of newspaper in their pen for they will not always wait to be taken outside and it will make clearing up much easier.

When puppies are about seven weeks old they should be wormed and, if you are keeping them, plans made for giving them their inoculations. At eight weeks they should be old enough to move on to their new homes.

teaspoonful of honey, half a teaspoonful of sodium bicarbonate and a heaped teaspoonful of a milk stimulant (not to be confused with puppy milk food) sold in capsules by pharmacists. You may have to hold her food bowl for a few days for she probably will not want to leave her box. For the next 24 hours her diet should be a milky one.

After the second day she should be fed three or four times daily, according to the size of the litter. Food for the medium size dog should include 580 g (1 lb) of raw meat and $\frac{1}{2}$ litre (1 pt) of milk each day supplemented by bone meal and a multivitamin source. Plenty of water is essential for her to produce sufficient milk.

After the third day let her have plenty of exercise which will stimulate her milk glands.

If you notice a puppy not getting on or sucking properly, pinch its skin up between your thumb and forefinger, and if it does not spring back almost at once, that puppy is not thriving. You can help it get a stronger hold on life by giving it a little extra nourishment from a bottle three times a day. Specially formulated puppy milk food is sold by pet stores and feeders are available on which the puppy can suck – but do not force milk down its throat or you may force it into its lungs. The mixture needs to be really warm when you put it in the feeder, for puppies hate a lukewarm bottle and will take it far hotter than you imagine – a little warmer than blood heat.

In some breeds it is the custom to dock, or shorten, the tail (although a growing number of people are

Above: The Old English Sheepdog is a breed which has become very popular. Unfortunately not all those who fell for the charms of the breed realized the time and money needed to rear and maintain in good health so large and heavily coated a dog. The black and white of the puppy coat will change to the grey or blue of the adult. **Top right:** A Pointer bitch allows her large litter to feed. Like a number of the other gundog breeds, Pointers are very fertile and tend to have a lot of puppies. **Bottom right:** Shih Tzus like these come in a wide variety of colours and make good watchdogs.

Overleaf left: The smaller terriers are cheeky game little dogs, usually as hard as nails and very active. They suit owners who like a lively animal but who do not expect too much in the way of slavish obedience. Most terriers would rather please themselves than their owners. This smooth-haired type is a Jack Russell, a non-pedigree dog but very popular. **Overleaf right:** These somewhat mournful-looking pups are Borzois but they have a lot of growing to do before they become adult. Good food and plenty of it must be given until their growing period is over.

Left: Active and inquisitive puppies can be unintentionally destructive and need continuous supervision. It is very natural for young animals to explore their surroundings, to dig and to chew. However, like young children they do not always know what is best for them.

Above: Puppies as young as this still need the company and security of their litter mates. Like all baby animals they need frequent small meals and the opportunity for lots of uninterrupted sleep in warm, dry surroundings.

Far left: The Golden Retriever is now one of the most popular breeds in Britain. None of the retrievers have a very long history, for they are all breeds which were developed in the nineteenth century to aid the sportsman by finding and bringing to hand dead and wounded game. Because they were bred originally for this particular purpose, all the retrievers are anxious to learn and easy to teach. Many Golden Retrievers work as guide dogs for the blind and many more are happy in the role of family pets.

Above: These five Pomeranians are all orange in colour, the most popular shade in a breed which can have a wide variety of coat colours. Pomeranians usually weigh 1·8–3 kg (4–7 lbs), though the smaller size is preferred and adults of 0·7 kg (1½ lbs) weight are not uncommon. The breed is a member of the Spitz family and, like most Spitz dogs, makes a bold and alert watchdog. Its vivacity and intelligence make it an excellent companion for the housebound or the lonely.

Near left: The spotted coat of the Dalmatian makes it one of the most easily recognized breeds and has led to its nickname of 'plum pudding dog'. We do not know where the Dalmatian came from but it seems very unlikely that it was Yugoslavia. The breed was a popular carriage dog in Victorian days, lending a fashionable air to a gentleman's barouche by trotting between the wheels or even between the lead horses. For those who like a strong, active dog, the Dalmatian is as tireless as they come. **Overleaf:** Three golden Cocker Spaniel puppies.

Left: Children learn a lot from keeping pets but need to be at least twelve years old before they can take full responsibility for an animal as demanding as a dog. The play of younger children and animals should always be supervised as one side can quite unwittingly hurt the other.

Above: Many people expect puppies to look like miniature editions of their parents. This is virtually never the case but the difference is most marked with long-haired breeds like these Standard Poodles.

Far left: Boxers are a German breed developed as guard and police dogs. They are fun-loving dogs which make excellent companions for energetic people, but they do need training and exercise to bring out the best in the relationship. This is one of the breeds which is cropped on the Continent and in America but has a natural dropped ear in Britain.

Left: Rough Collies have long been public favourites, particularly after the success of the *Lassie* films and books. The working collie is a Scottish dog and the more glamorous Rough Collie was developed from working stock in the late nineteenth century. Rough Collies are kept world wide as pets. They are easy to train but have lost the instinctive drive necessary for a successful working sheepdog, a field in which they have been superseded by the Border Collie.

Below: The Whippet's fragile looks belie the breed's strength and determination when coursing a hare. It has the fastest acceleration of any breed.

Learning to obey

You own a dog to give you pleasure, not to be a nuisance, and it is the dog which must learn to fit into your life, rather than the other way around. Of course, you must begin by choosing a dog whose needs are matched to your own but, given that is so, both sides will find an obedient relationship a happier one – and so will anyone else with whom they come into contact. Safety, as well as convenience, demands that a dog be taught to come when called, to follow to heel and to stay where he is told. Some people like to think of their pets as 'almost human' and imagine it is this quality that makes them understand what is wanted of them – but such anthropomorphic ideas must be forgotten. A dog is a dog and deserves to be treated as one, not as a substitute person, and it is his natural dog instincts which make it possible to teach him to be obedient.

The dog is one of the easiest animals to train, not because he has a superior brain – the cat is probably more intelligent – but because he is a pack animal with a strong instinct to follow a leader, while the cat likes to be its own master and make its own decisions and, although it may decide that life is more comfortable if it fits in with some of our plans, it is untrainable in the way we expect a dog to be. The dog will be willing, indeed sometimes anxious, to accept a human master as his leader, while the cat will only accept him as a friend. In fact, contrary to common belief, greater intelligence does not make a dog trainable. Indeed, exceptional intelligence is the cause of many dogs being quite untrainable. Most difficult and disobedient dogs are very intelligent, and in some cases the whole problem arises from the fact that their intelligence surpasses that of their owners!

There is a snag. Dogs vary enormously in their degree of dominance and submissiveness, from the born leader to the lowest member of the pack – and the same applies to human beings. If a dominant dog is under the control of a submissive owner he may well prove quite untrainable, although he could turn out to be an excellent subject with a dominant owner. This unbalance is probably the major cause of dog/owner problems and the first essential for successful training is likely to lie in finding the right dog to train.

Training depends partly upon the strength of a dog's own instincts and in the centuries during which men have bred dogs for particular purposes these have been deliberately strengthened or weakened by careful selection. As well as the degrees of dominance in individual dogs, some types, as a breed; are characteristically more submissive and willing to learn, while in other breeds the majority are dominant and anxious to lead rather than to be led. The basic instinct which drives a Greyhound to chase a hare is the same as that which leads a sheepdog to work sheep, but selective breeding has produced various breeds of sheepdog in which the majority are willing, even eager, to be trained. The same applies to gun dogs. But with Greyhounds, Afghans and their like it is a very different case. Once a hound has been unleashed to pursue its quarry its master has no part to play, except to follow it – it is the dog which leads. A hound which is too submissive will not be good at its job and as a result hounds, and terriers too, are usually much more difficult to train than gundogs and sheepdogs – although this does not mean that they cannot be taught to be obedient and well-behaved with more effort and a dominant owner.

Within a household a dog will often obey some members of the family but not others. In recent years, trainers have tried to study and practise the methods used by the canine pack leaders, with very successful results.

The most important lesson for the human owner to learn from the canine pack leader is that by gaining the respect of his subordinates he will also gain their affection and loyalty. A good pack leader commands respect without bullying. He has no need to keep proving how big and strong he is, and therefore does not put himself in a position to be challenged. The bully who rules by force may obtain implicit obedience, but at the loss of friendship or affection.

Left: The smooth Fox Terrier is one of the smartest and the most trouble-free of the terrier breeds. It is gay, lively and active and has a coat which requires little in the way of attention.

65

Unfortunately a large number of trainers (including very successful trainers in trials and competitions of various types) adopt the latter policy. Never having trained by any other method, they have no idea of the pleasure they are losing in not having a dog which works *with* its master rather than *for* him – a dog which is a good servant *and* a loyal friend.

Dogs do not reason as we do. They learn by association of ideas. We learn in exactly the same way, especially when we are young. A five-year old child will understand you when you warn him 'If you put your finger near the fire you will get burnt', but a year-old baby will not and has to be prevented from going near the fire by a fireguard. If, accidentally, he gets burnt he is unlikely to need warning about fires again. He will associate the painful experience with the fire and avoid it for a very long time.

Naturally, a dog tends to repeat the actions which he finds pleasant and to refrain from doing the things he finds unpleasant, so in training we try to make it pleasant for the dog to do the things we want him to do and unpleasant for him to do the things we don't want him to do. We must be careful not to build up the wrong associations accidentally. It is a strange fact that if a child gets bitten by a dog he is excused of being afraid of dogs for the rest of his life, but if a dog is kicked by a child he is considered stupid to be afraid of children and nasty if he is aggressive towards them.

We can learn a great deal about how to train a dog by watching the way in which a bitch treats her puppies. If they pester her she growls at them. Most puppies will respond to the sound and stop pulling their mother's tail or ear, or whatever else they were doing which annoyed her. Sometimes a dominant puppy ignores her and then the bitch will snap at him – often quite severely – and he will immediately stop. Usually the bitch then licks and caresses the puppy to stop him crying but he will remember what has happened and next time he will associate the sound of a growl with a nasty snap and stop whatever he is doing. If dog owners follow this simple pattern they usually find it works and the puppy quickly learns the signs that indicate disapproval.

The first thing that any puppy must learn is his name: and the choice of name should always be made with care to ensure that it is one that is easily recognized when called and cannot be confused with

Above left: The dog always works at the trainer's left-hand side. This yellow Labrador sits happily beside its owner, demonstrating the confident relationship there should be between dog and master. This sort of working partnership between a boy and his dog is of immense benefit to both. **Left**: Teaching your dog to sit on command is one of the basic steps to an obedient animal. **Right**: This black Labrador is learning to stay when left by his owner. Patient repetition produces success and regular practice ensures that the dog is reliable.

any of the orders you may wish to give. Use the name from the moment that the puppy becomes yours, and always speak it in a pleasant tone of voice, while correction and reprove should be given in a harsh, growling tone.

Toilet training should have been achieved by simple conditioning, as described in an earlier chapter, and is a matter of controlling nature, not of obeying you. The first obedience lesson will be to come when called. All training should begin in a place where the young dog feels secure and surrounded by familiar things, so that he is not distracted by the need to investigate the place, and, to teach him to come when called, see that he is somewhere from which it is impossible for him to run off. If he will not come to you in the house or garden you have small chance of his coming to you in a park or open field. With a new dog or puppy that knows nothing, wait until he shows signs of coming to you, crouch down, extend a hand with fingers moving and call him by his name followed by 'Come', 'Here' or whatever word you intend using thereafter. Remember that it is not what you say but rather how you say it that the dog responds to, so use the nicest, friendliest tone of voice that you can manage. Almost certainly the puppy will come to you. Then you can offer him a tit-bit and make a great fuss of him – indeed, many trainers believe that treats are quite unnecessary and that praise and affection are all the reward that a dog should need. Next time he hears the same sound (his name followed by 'Here') in the same

tone of voice he will associate it with approval and should come to you. But he will not associate it with anything if the whole family keep repeating his name and calling him from all directions at the same time. All that will teach him is to ignore his name completely, just as he ignores a sound which is constantly repeated on the radio.

Never call a dog to you to give him reproof or punishment. If you do he will associate the punishment with coming to you and think that that was wrong. Owners who, on a dog's return, attempt to punish him for running away only teach their dogs *not* to come when called. A young or untrained dog associates correction or reward with what he is doing or is about to do, not with what he has done. What is on his mind is what matters, not what his body is doing. That is why a bright young dog, punished when he returns to his owner, quickly learns that when he hears his master's voice calling in an angry tone the safest thing to do is to keep well out of reach. Therefore remember always to praise him well when he comes back, no matter what he has done.

Once a puppy has learned his name, but *not* before, he can be taught the meaning of 'No!' When he does something which is forbidden – chewing the carpet, for example – you should say 'No' to him in a harsh growling tone (never shout – the puppy has better hearing than you). A sensitive puppy will probably react to this growl and stop chewing, whereupon you should praise him by stroking him and encouraging

him in a friendly tone. If he does not respond to the growl, follow immediately with correction which, for a puppy of this age, can be a light tap on the nose or gripping the scruff of his neck. As soon as the puppy responds, praise him well. A lively puppy will probably take some time to learn, but repeat the whole performance more severely each time until he gives up.

Every dog needs a collar to carry his identification tag (although tattooing is now being used by some owners as a more permanent means of identification), and a lead to control his movements when in public. A collar and lead are also essential for training. Collars are available in flat leather with a buckle fastening, narrow round leather (with fancy studs and paste jewels for such toy breeds as miniature poodles), and in nylon, which is strong, durable, washable, and very light for the dog to wear. Chain collars are usually 'slip collars', and are often used for training, but a slip collar should never be left on a dog, for the ring can easily catch upon something and strangle him. For general use a light collar will be more comfortable for the dog, and even that should be taken off at night. Your name and address can be engraved upon a disc or plate attached to the collar, or written upon a slip of paper carried in a barrel-like receptacle attached to the collar – a method which enables you easily to change the address if you take your dog on holiday with you. Leads can be of leather or nylon (which has the advantage that it takes up less space and can be rolled up in the pocket). Chain leads are not very practical and should not be used unless the dog chews through leather or nylon ones. Leads should be of a reasonable length, because short ones encourage a dog to pull, and they should have a strong clip fastening to attach them to the collar.

Puppies of six to ten weeks of age need little training to accept a collar and lead, although as they get older they will need additional training to teach them to walk beside you. An older dog can sometimes be very obstinate and demand drastic action, probably trying to resist wearing a collar and lead at all. When the dog stops fighting to free himself from them attempt to coax him to come to you, meanwhile pulling upon the lead. If he will not come he must be dragged – but continue coaxing him with a gentle voice until he responds, and do not forget to praise him when he does.

The next lesson is to teach the dog to 'sit'. One method is to hold the collar firmly in one hand while pressing the dog's rump gently down with the other

Top right: A choke chain or slip collar is nearly always used for training. It must be put on properly and used correctly to get the maximum benefit. The ring which slides free along the chain should always come from under the dog's neck. **Bottom right**: This Great Dane is being rewarded by praise. **Far right**: A slip lead for puppies.

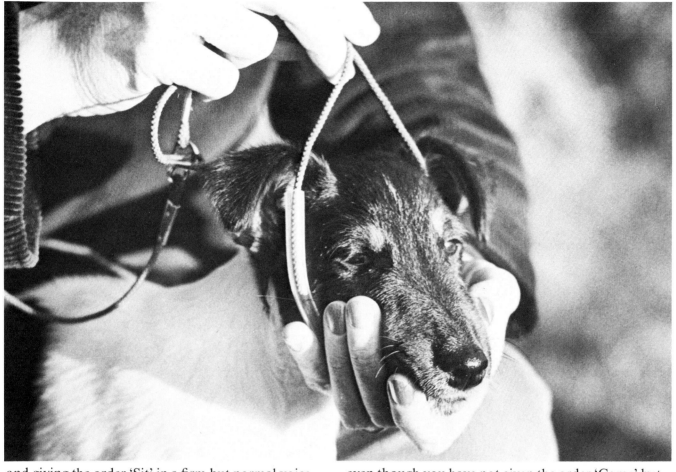

and giving the order 'Sit' in a firm but normal voice. Hold the dog down for a few moments, stroking and soothing him at the same time, then move slightly away and say 'Come'. He will probably have moved even before you give the order but it is as well to associate the end of the sit with an order from the start. Repeat the process several times then try it holding his collar but without pushing him down. If he sits give him plenty of praise and try it again. If he does not carry out the instruction do not scold him – simply push him down. Next day try the lesson again and go on to give the order without even holding his collar.

For most pet owners it does not matter whether a dog is taught to sit or to lie since the main purpose is to get him to stay in one place in a fairly relaxed condition. However the 'Sit' can easily be converted to 'Lie' by placing the hand which was pushing down the rump behind the dog's knees and, while giving the order 'Down', pulling the front legs forward and pressing down on the shoulders. Another way of teaching the 'Down' – especially if you do not want to bother with the intermediate 'Sit' – is to stand by the dog with the lead in your right hand and falling in a loop from the hand back up to the dog's collar. Then put your left foot on the loop, at the same time placing your left hand on the dog's shoulder, and pull the lead through your instep with the right hand as you give the order 'Down'.

The next stage is to teach the dog to stay. At first the dog will probably follow you when you move away,

even though you have not given the order 'Come' but told him 'Stay'. If he does return at once, say 'No', and put him back into the sit or lie position. Gradually, as he gets the idea, you can move farther and farther away from him and even around a corner out of sight. During training do *not* give the order 'Come' when the dog is in the stay position without going up to him first or you may produce a confused reaction.

The stay is probably the most useful of all obedience exercises, for a dog lying down cannot bite someone walking close by, nor jump up and leave muddy marks on the best suit of a non-doggy guest. Even if he will not come to you, provided that he stays there you can go to him and attach a lead. Perhaps most important of all is that teaching a dog to lie down quietly beside you for long periods will do his temperament a lot of good. Indeed it is the only way of steadying down an over-excitable dog.

A choke collar makes it easier to teach a dog to walk to heel. Put it on so that it will fall slack if you are not applying pressure. If the dog walks by your side in the correct position the collar will be quite comfortable but if he pulls or hangs back you should apply pressure. If you hold the lead in front of your body by the hand on the opposite side to the dog it leaves the near hand free for praise or correction.

Dogs which become a nuisance by persistently jumping up can be discouraged if you simply raise your knee, which will push them off-balance as they

Left: Many dogs enjoy doing tricks. The attention and praise they receive is a satisfying reward. This miniature long-haired Dachshund begs for sympathy. **Above**: Training a dog to attack on command should be left strictly to the experts.

do it. If they attempt to mount a person's arms, legs or a piece of furniture – an embarrassing habit of many highly-sexed adolescent dogs – they should be pulled off and slapped across the flank.

A dog who has learned these lessons should be easy to control both on and off the lead, at home and out of doors. When you take your dog out in the street you should always encourage him to sit whenever he reaches the edge of a kerb then, should he accidentally go out into the street at any time without a lead he will be less likely to rush across the road without your order. Even if you always make sure he is on a lead when in traffic areas, which you should certainly do, this will avoid any risk of him attempting to cross the road and causing an accident.

Every dog should have this basic training and it forms the groundwork before the specialized training of working dogs whether as gundogs, guard dogs, guide or police dogs. But even if your dog is a pet who does not have to earn his living he will enjoy taking his training very much further and will probably master a whole repertoire of games and tricks.

Retrieving a ball is instinctive behaviour with many dogs, a response to their hunting past. Many puppies will run after a ball and pick it up, sometimes bringing it back and sometimes running off to play with it. The first time he sees the ball 'running away', the puppy will usually lollop after it only half seriously. But if the game is continued, he will quickly become more and more enthusiastic until he can be relied on to fetch a ball every time it is thrown. This is one instinct which can grow stronger with usage to the extent of becoming overdeveloped and many dogs are completely obsessed by balls, sticks, stones or anything else they can carry.

There seems to come a particular point in a puppy's development when such instincts surface, whether they flourish depends partly upon the strength of the inherent interest and partly on the encouragement that is given. A puppy which has shown no previous inclination to retrieve may suddenly decide to do so. If encouraged at this stage the instinct will quickly grow stronger, but if discouraged it will weaken and possibly die out altogether. A dog which has never been allowed to play with a ball as a puppy is very unlikely to do so as an adult. Some dogs, particularly the gun dog breeds, have very strong retrieving instincts which will survive under very adverse conditions. At the opposite extreme, other dogs are so completely devoid of the retrieving instinct that it is impossible to persuade them to pick up anything at all. In between are the majority of dogs, which require training to develop the retrieving instinct or to keep it under control, as the case may be.

Although many dogs hardly need to be taught to 'Fetch', they will probably not be so ready to give up what they have brought. 'Drop' should be gently said while removing the object from the dog's mouth and stroking him approvingly. Do not shout or get the slightest bit annoyed, and do not try to pull or grab the object, or he may think that this is a new tugging game. In fact, do not pull the object at all. Simply hold it and pull the dog backwards, away from it.

Most dogs learn to beg without any difficulty. Some will beg almost instinctively and others will pick up the idea if you hold a titbit just out of their reach, but not so high that they feel encouraged to jump for it. Some dogs can learn to balance for quite long periods and even to 'dance' upon two legs, but these are tricks that should not be taught until the dog is adult, for they place considerable strain upon the back and leg muscles and could lead to deformities in the young puppy.

Jumping obstacles is easily taught by calling the dog with a small obstacle between you and him which he cannot avoid, gradually raising its height as the dog's confidence grows. As a variation the dog can also be taught to jump over an outstretched arm or through a hoop. Many dogs will learn to carry your newspaper or, among the larger breeds, a light basket of shopping, to find a hidden object, to shake a paw and many other tricks. Often some accidental piece of behaviour can be encouraged so that the dog will happily make it part of a game which he will play to win your approval as much as for the inherent pleasure it will give him.

The specialized training of dogs for use by the armies in the First World War, and their employment as police and guide dogs since, have made people aware of just how highly dogs can be trained and many ordinary dog owners now take their pets to advanced obedience classes and compete in obedience trials. In England well over 30 obedience championship shows are held each year and more than 400 trial meetings at which dogs do not compete for titles, while in the United States the American Kennel Club licenses many hundreds of trials which attract more than 50,000 entries. In America crossbreeds do not compete in the official competitions but in Britain mongrels and pure-breds, which cannot be registered for conformation competitions, can be registered for obedience only and enter in the trials which the Kennel Club controls.

Obedience trials are now worldwide, although rules differ from country to country and in some places there are separate classes for different kinds of working dog. The exercises in which dogs must show their paces include free heel, drop at command during recall, retrieve on the flat, retrieve over a high jump, three minute sit and five minute stay with the handler out of sight. There are also competitions in selecting and retrieving various articles, in retrieving unknown objects on hand signal instructions from the handler and tracking tests.

Obedience classes – at which the owners learn how to teach their dogs – are often run by obedience clubs for the general public whose dogs might not be eligible for competition. They are a valuable way of training mongrels and household pets to become better canine citizens and are a source of pleasure for owners and dogs alike.

Below: A guide dog for the blind has to learn to judge both the height and the width of obstacles.

Guards, guides & shepherd dogs

The dog has always been prepared to defend his own and as part of man's pack will defend his leader and his possessions. At times dogs have played an offensive rather than a defensive role, going into battle as part of the fighting forces, and their pugnacity formed the basis of such entertainments as bear baiting and rat catching as well as being set to fight with other dogs for the sport of their owners. Fortunately few people would find such a spectacle an entertainment in our own days and many of the breeds developed for such battles have gentle and stable temperaments with those they know and trust, and make excellent family dogs as well as good watchdogs and guards. The frequently forbidding looks of the Bulldog and the Mastiff belie one half of their personality.

It is not only the large breeds that have proved effective guards, many small breeds have done the job for centuries. The Schipperke was used to repel boarders from Flemish barges a century and a half ago and can still be seen riding on tradesman's vans, guarding them while deliveries are made. The Keeshond from the Netherlands was another barge dog and the little Lhasa Apso, now becoming popular as a pet, is a courageous guard dog from Tibet. The Dalmatian, usually thought of as an ornament to a gentleman's carriage, was in fact primarily a guard dog and at one time was also used in war.

Many of the breeds which we think of as sheepdogs were also originally mainly guard dogs. It was their job to protect the flocks from wolves, bears and thieves. In some countries, where the practice is to 'fold' sheep in hurdle enclosures, the dogs must act as both herders and guard dogs. Usually this kind of dog has been expected to drive the sheep rather than to round them up and would be used for taking the sheep – or cattle – to market as well as watching them on the farm.

In countries like Britain, where large predators were exterminated long ago and there is no need to 'fold' the sheep at night, they are left to roam the hills and pastures day and night. Their shepherd needs a dog which can round up his flock and control it with precision – a real herding dog. Originating mainly in Britain, and thence taken around the world, these sheepdogs have had their herding instinct developed from their basic hunting instinct, from which it is only a slight variation. In any hunting pack, there are dogs which will run around the quarry and turn it back into the pack. By breeding from these dogs it was possible to produce dogs with a natural instinct to run around other animals. However it is vital that these dogs do not attack and kill their quarry and although working sheepdogs still retain the instinct to hunt and kill, they have been trained not to do so when working. This is only possible when the submissive instinct is strong enough to counter-balance the very strong hunting instinct. In developing the herding breeds, Man has therefore bred for a strong submissive instinct. Generally speaking, dogs from the herding breeds are more easily trained than those from the hound and terrier groups.

More than 70 different types of sheep and cattle herding dogs exist today – more than half of them in Europe. Britain alone has nine breeds, seven of them recognized by the Kennel Club and the other two, the Border and Welsh Collies, although unrecognized for showing, have stud books which are zealously guarded by the International Sheepdog Society. Australia, South America, Africa and the Middle East all have their own herding dogs but North America has not produced an indigenous breed.

Sheepdogs, world wide, vary enormously in type, each being adapted to suit the kind of work expected of it and the type of terrain on which it has to perform. In Poland, for instance, there is the Tatra Mountain Sheepdog, reaching at least 700 mm (28 in) at the shoulder, while the Little Sheepdog of the Polish valleys attains a height of a mere 300 mm (12 in).

The majority of the herding breeds are very sweet-tempered, reliable and trustworthy towards their owners and their family, but at the same time make it clear that they are ready to protect the flock, home and family, to the death if necessary. (Indeed some individuals can become over-protective, like the

Pyrenean Mountain Dog who used to jealously guard his mistress from her potential boyfriends!) On a farm they will often be an 'all-purpose' dog, even to the extent of being gundog, retriever and poacher in addition to their other duties.

The true sheepdog's character can be quite exceptional. It is rare to encounter any of the herding breeds that are not highly intelligent, sensible and sensitive, as well as having an innate desire to please. Their brains seem to function and reason in almost the same way as our own. Sheepdogs are strongly telepathic, much more so than the other breeds. They have a strong sense of possession and a great sense of right and wrong – especially when it is *we* who are right or wrong! They are extremely sensitive to our moods and their understanding of them is quite uncanny.

Whether the dog is at its daily work, training to compete for trials or just being a family pet, his mission in life is to meet with approval, and he goes about his task of trying to please in an unobtrusive manner. If a dog is kept as a pet and cannot carry out his natural duties it is essential to help him to fulfil himself. He must never be bereft of human companionship, for his fertile mind will go to seed and he will become sad, maybe even untrustworthy. An intelligent dog who is bored is often a troublesome dog.

If you have never watched these dogs in difficult terrain or in sheepdog trials, you cannot fully appreciate what they can do. Their brilliance has to be seen to be believed. These are not dogs trained by rote. They respond to their master's commands yet use their own brains too. In mountainous country the dog is often out of sight of his master. He has to use his own intelligence, not just instinct, and solve many difficult problems for himself.

Herding breeds do not all work alike. Sheepdogs working in the plains may lope along hour after hour while others, which must be smaller and more nimble, tend their charges among mountain crags and gullies. All must be trained, but each must also have a tremendous amount of inherited ability and they are often trained as much by their parents as by their masters.

A man with a clever dog can handle with the utmost efficiency large flocks and herds which could not possibly be handled by several men without a dog's aid. In these days of mechanized farming the shepherding breeds are happily one group of animals which can never be superceded by machine.

The first sheepdog trials in Britain were held in October 1873 in Wales and continued annually, with increases each year both in attendance and the number of competitors. In 1876 the first trials were held in England, and Scotland followed suit in the same year. Six years after the first trials Queen Victoria witnessed a private trial at Bala and this led to the Bala Trials becoming the most important of the annual competitions. Interest in the trials gradually increased until the First World War, when there was a break, but after this they picked up again and not only spread throughout Britain but became increasingly popular in all English speaking countries. Trials throughout the world are now held under the rules of the International Sheepdog Society, as they are in Britain.

In recent years the breeding and training of sheepdogs has become much more scientific and sophisticated. Sheepdog trials have had much to do with this and have resulted in a specialist dog bred for the purpose, now known generally as the Border Collie, deriving the name from the border between Scotland and England. The International Sheepdog Society refers to this breed as a working sheepdog and the studbook has sections for rough-coated, smooth-coated and beardie-coated. In Scotland the Border Collie is also called the 'trial-bred dog' or 'creeper', a most apt name for describing its style of working. It is the style of working, rather than its appearance, which makes this dog different from all other breeds and types of sheepdog. The Border Collie has what is known as a 'strong eye', enabling him to 'hold' a single sheep with his 'eye'. What he does, in fact, is to creep steadily and stealthily towards his 'prey', never for an instant relaxing his menacing stare. The sheep becomes almost mesmerized and either stands still or moves backwards. The 'eye' is so strong that it even affects people.

Dogs cannot be taught to work in this way, they must be bred to do it. The 'strong eye' is merely an exaggeration of the wild dog's natural instinct to stalk its prey. Until they are trained, the majority of good young dogs follow that instinct a stage further by grabbing hold of the sheep, but as their submissive instinct is also very highly developed it is not usually very difficult to teach them not to do this. The attitude adopted by the strong-eyed sheepdog is exactly the same as that adopted by pointers and setters, and a sheepdog will set at a sheep which he scents but cannot see, for example, a sheep buried in snow, just as a bird dog sets at a grouse.

'Strong eye' is by no means the only quality of the modern Border Collie. He is a wide-running, stylish worker and, when handled properly, can surpass any other type of sheepdog for certain types of work. But, because these are such high-powered dogs, they do require very delicate handling. Bred carefully, the herding instinct in the Border Collie can only be described as over developed. They will literally work, or try to work, anything from a mouse to an elephant and, without training and adequate exercise, the Border Collie is one of the most unsuitable of all dogs to keep as a pet.

Although not recognized by the British Kennel Club, the Border Collie is shown in Australian dog shows, and it is from Australia that the Kelpie comes – to stands alongside the Border as the two most

Right: The Maremma is an Italian sheepdog which has been in use in the wilder parts of the Apennines for many centuries. It is a guard dog rather than a herding dog and was expected to keep the flocks safe from both predators and thieves. Like a number of the larger sheepdogs which were used as guards, the Maremma is white. This may have been so that it could be distinguished more easily from attacking wolves. A white dog is also considered by some to be less likely to panic the sheep and the colour therefore allowed the Maremma to guard the flocks more closely. Though they are handsome dogs, the breed is not well known outside Italy. **Below:** The Bearded Collie is an old Scottish breed of sheepdog which was used widely for cattle droving. It had become very scarce before being recognized in 1949 by the British Kennel Club as purebred. Now Bearded Collies are widely kept as family dogs and show dogs by people who appreciate their energetic nature and shaggy charm. They can be any shade of grey or brown and they usually have white collie markings. Like all the sheepdogs with a long history of close association with man, the Beardie is an exceptionally responsive dog to human companionship.

important working sheepdogs in the world. Unlike its British ancestors, the Kelpie has stayed in his native land where he proves his value on the great sheep stations. It is believed that all Kelpies are descended from one bitch, 'King's Kelpie', born of imported Scottish stock, which won Australia's first sheepdog trial in 1872, but some Australian ingredients no doubt went into the creation of a sheepdog to work under local conditions, which demand a dog that can work thousands rather than hundreds of sheep, ending up with a tough, independent working dog showing as much 'eye' as a good Border Collie.

The Australian Cattle Dog came into existence at about the same time as the Kelpie and from much the same ancestry, though with Dingo blood added to increase the toughness of the already tough Scottish stock. Dogs, such as the Corgi, had worked cattle in Britain long before Australia was discovered, but 100 head of cattle was considered quite a big drove and there were hedges and ditches around the fields and along the old drove roads. In New South Wales and Victoria a 'mob' of cattle can be over 1,000 head, while the 'paddocks' can run into thousands of acres. The cattle are controlled by dogs working alongside mounted 'jackaroos', or cowboys. Weaklings have no place in this type of farming and, just to be able to survive, dogs need to be really tough. Explicit commands cannot be given in the same way as they are with a dog working at a sheepdog trial or on a quiet hillside in Wales or Scotland, so the Cattle Dog has to be able to think for himself and use his own initiative. The result is an extremely intelligent animal with exceptional agility of both mind and body.

The herding breeds are not confined to dogs which work sheep and cattle. In many parts of the world dogs work with goats, pigs, reindeer and other animals. In fact the true pastoral breeds are dogs of enormous adaptability and as well as efficiently carrying out their natural work they can be trained to do very different things, although they are happiest using their strong herding instinct.

The German Shepherd Dog (the Alsatian) is now probably better known for its many other roles than as a herding dog. German Shepherds formed the majority of the dogs trained by the German Army before the First World War, and today they work with the police forces of the world and serve as rescue and guide dogs. Unfortunately some people using German

Shepherds as security guards have been glad to encourage any savagery in their nature, and lack of selection by unscrupulous breeders seeking to profit from the popularity of the breed has also led to some dogs of bad character which have attracted very adverse publicity to the breed. Until recently the import of German Shepherd Dogs into Australia was totally banned on the grounds that they worried sheep – a topsy-turvy situation for a dog reared as a shepherd. These dogs do have a nervous trait in their make-up and a nervous dog the size of the German Shepherd can be a dangerous dog. It is important that they have firm owners who can control them properly and that their abilities are used. Essentially working dogs, they can become very frustrated if not given anything to do. As a result there have been tragic cases of people being mauled – and even killed – by dogs not under proper control. However, with correct handling the German Shepherd is a very good dog indeed.

Dogs were used again by the military during the Second World War and their contribution exceeded

Left: The Border Collie is the world's premier working sheepdog. Here a Border demonstrates control over a defiant ewe. These dogs must not bite and depend a great deal on determination and strength of 'eye'. **Above right**: The Tervueren is one of three very similar varieties of Belgian Sheepdog. **Right**: Welsh Corgis were originally cattle dogs. Their short legs meant that they could nip the heels of uncooperative bullocks and be too low to the ground to be caught by the retaliatory kicks. These are the Pembrokeshire variety of Corgi.

all expectations. Patrol dogs were used to give warning of enemy approach and because of their vastly superior sense of smell and hearing they could detect a hidden person when a man would have no idea that he was there. These dogs had to work silently since the slightest whimper might warn the enemy of their whereabouts. They 'pointed' their quarry just as a pointer indicates a grouse.

Guard dogs were used to protect airfields and ammunition dumps and both the Army and the Air Force continue to use them for this purpose in peacetime. Dogs have been trained as mine detectors and have traced mines buried 3 m (10 ft) deep in shifting sand. Messenger dogs were also used with conspicuous success. They were trained to work with two handlers, one of whom went out on patrol while the other stayed at base. The dogs carried messages between the two handlers in a special collar. In many cases they worked over ground where a man could easily have been spotted, and, of course, they could run faster. Rescue dogs were trained to search for wounded servicemen and, on the home front, to find people buried beneath rubble during bombing raids. One German Shepherd rescued over 200 people during the London blitz. Dogs were also used in prisoner of war camps, both as guards and for tracking escaped prisoners. The number of Allied prisoners caught by German dogs far exceeded the number of German prisoners caught by British dogs.

The vast majority of service dogs today are German Shepherd Dogs. They can be trained for the work, are about the right size and have coats which are easily cared for yet provide protection from the weather.

The use of dogs for police work was also pioneered in Germany. Most people imagine a police dog as an animal that is ever ready to tear them limb from limb. Police dogs are taught 'man work' and are expected to protect their handlers or to catch a criminal running away but they rarely have the opportunity to do either. Today's police forces also use dogs to search for drugs, explosives and firearms – a task at which the Labrador Retriever has proved to

Top left: The Groenendael is the best known of the Belgian Sheepdogs. It has been used both as a police and army dog and makes an excellent guard dog. **Left:** Any sizeable dog makes an effective deterrent should trouble threaten, but a well-trained dog is more effective still. **Top right:** The Rottweiler is a German police and army dog which is being kept in increasing numbers in Britain and America. This dog combines obvious power and strength with agility. The short, smooth coat is always black and tan. **Near right:** The Bouvier Des Flandres is one of the French sheepdog breeds. A rugged, powerful animal with a coarse, dark coat, the Bouvier has also been used for army and police work. **Far right:** For those who can afford to keep a giant dog, the Great Dane makes the best of guards.

be most accomplished – but the greatest part of a police dog's work is in finding people or clues to their whereabouts. These people may be dangerous criminals, escaped lunatics or lost children: whoever it may be the first essential a civilian police dog has to learn is that it only bites when told to do so. For military and police work both dog and handler must undergo intensive training and regular refresher courses. The dogs are taught to arrest a man by seizing his arm, which is padded to avoid injury. The only time a police dog is ever allowed to attack without being commanded by the handler is if the handler is attacked unexpectedly.

It was the successful use of dogs during the First World War that suggested a more specialized role to help alleviate some of the misery the war had caused. In 1916 large-scale training began in Germany to provide guide dogs for the many people who had been blinded. Sightless people had used dogs as guides for centuries and the first known attempt to train dogs to lead the blind was made by a Paris hospital in the eighteenth century, but it was not until 1916 that the task was tackled in a major way. Gradually the idea spread around the world. Mrs Dorothy Harrison Eustace, an American living in Switzerland, saw and was impressed by the work that was being done and founded the first Seeing Eye organization. This led to the creation of the Master Eye Institute in America in 1926, which was followed by other organizations, including the British Guide Dogs for the Blind Association, founded in 1931.

Dogs of many breeds have been trained as guides. German Shepherds, Labradors and Golden Retrievers are the most usual, although one guide was a pure-bred Malamute and numerous crossbred bitches are taken into training every year and give faithful service. The animals are obtained by gift, by purchase or are bred at the training centre, and it is their temperament that is all-important. There must be no trace of nervousness, and the dog must be friendly – though not the type that fawns upon strangers. He must pay intelligent attention to the human voice, use his own initiative and not show aggression towards other animals.

The puppies are 'walked' by volunteers from twelve weeks to ten months of age, and these temporary owners are expected to housetrain the puppies and familiarize them with traffic and riding in buses and on trains. If they still prove suitable for the work, they are then trained at a centre by skilled professionals who have to teach them to allow for the size of their master wherever they go – both his extra width in going past something and his height if going through an arch or under an overhanging branch. Unlike any other trained dog they must also learn to ignore some instructions, refusing to cross a road until traffic is clear or to advance in any situation which could be dangerous for their owner.

Training takes from four to six months and then the dogs are matched to a suitable blind owner, who must also be taught how to control the dog and how to follow his guidance through the handle of the special harness. The blind person does not meet the dog at first. For two or three days he learns to give the basic commands with his sighted trainer at the other end of the harness. During this time the trainer can assess his student's temperament, reactions and general character before selecting the dog which will make the best match. Together student and dog spend a month training within the centre, finally visiting shops, travelling on public transport and learning how to negotiate obstacles, busy conditions and traffic as a team. The blind person will also be given training in the care of the dog and, after they have left to start their new life together, there are follow-up visits from the centre staff to make sure there are no problems.

Sadly a guide dog's active life is usually shorter than that of his owner (or rather her owner, since bitches are usually chosen for the work because they are less likely to be distracted by other dogs and their scents) but when the time comes for a dog to retire her owner goes to the top of the waiting list for a replacement.

The various guide dog organizations are dependent upon voluntary donations and anyone with a little money to spare would have to look a long way for a worthier cause to support.

Dogs also carry out valuable service for the welfare of man in alpine rescue teams, finding the victims buried by an avalance or other disaster. Even today they are still used in arctic regions as a means of transport but elsewhere their role as draught animals is almost a thing of the past. Europe produced several big, strong breeds of the Mastiff type which could pull amazing loads but they did not equal the efficiency of a team of Huskies.

At one time there were an estimated 175,000 draught dogs in Belgium where they were the main form of transport for bakers, grocers and other tradesmen. All had to hold licences and it is doubtful if any other beast of burden was surrounded by so many rules and regulations.

Draught dogs were banned from the streets of London in 1839 because of their incessant barking, and from the public highways throughout Britain in 1854, and their use is now illegal. It would appear that these dogs were pretty badly treated but it does not follow that it is cruel to put a dog in harness, any more than it is to harness a horse. Either can be very cruel if the harness fits badly, or if the animal strains itself with loads that are too heavy. Most dogs enjoy pulling, as can be seen by anyone who watches the many dogs who tow their owners along the road on a lead.

Right: The Old English Sheepdog is a large, rumbustious dog. Though its square build gives it a clumsy appearance, it is an agile dog with a surprising turn of speed. The coat needs a great deal of attention if it is not to become matted.

Above: The Pyrenean Mountain Dog, or Great Pyrenees as it is called in America, is one of the most popular of the giant breeds. **Top right**: A shepherd depends on his dogs to do work that he could not possibly accomplish himself.
Bottom right: The work done by Arctic sledge dogs is probably the hardest undertaken by any breed of dog. Up until now all polar travel depended on them.

Overleaf: The Rough Collie is a glamourized version of the working Scottish Collie which was a general purpose farm dog with a sensible temperament, a broad skull and not so heavy a coat. Show enthusiasts took them up and altered them to give them more elegance, narrower, more refined skulls and a more luxurious coat. They have been favourite pets ever since.

Far left: The Shetland Sheepdog is a Rough Collie in miniature. Though their ancestors were to be found in the Shetland Isles, herding the small island sheep, the present-day breed are much more glamorous and dainty than their forebears.

Top left: The Cardigan Welsh Corgi is the lesser-known of the two Corgi breeds. It was also a farm and cattle dog and is slightly heavier in build than its Pembrokeshire cousin. The Cardigan has a magnificent bushy tail and is very often dark brindle in colour.

Bottom left: The Briard comes from France where it was originally a sheepdog. However, its intelligence and willingness meant that it adapted easily to army and police work. It is now found in Britain and America as a show and companion dog.

Far left: The Komondor is a sheepdog from the plains of Hungary. Like the Italian Maremma, the French Pyrenean and the Hungarian Kuvasz, it is another large white breed used for guarding rather than herding the flocks of semi-wild sheep. The most remarkable thing about the Komondor is its coat which, in the adult, is an enormous mass of felted cords and mats. This provides complete protection against extremes of weather and most accidental injuries.

Top left: The modern British Bulldog bears little relation to the bull-baiting ancestor from which it takes its name. The dog is now an amiable, heavy-breathing animal in marked contrast to its savage but active forbears.

Below: Teaching police and guard dogs to attack is one of the more difficult parts of their training. Few well-balanced dogs want to bite man and those that do so readily are usually too nervous to be dependable as working animals. Here a 'criminal' wearing padded, protective clothing teases and threatens a German Shepherd to get the dog to attack on the handler's command.

Top left: Two Rottweilers wait to compete in a test designed to demonstrate their working ability and steadiness of temperament.
Bottom left: The Samoyed takes its name from the nomadic Russian tribe who used the dog to herd their reindeer, guard their camps, pull their sledges and provide hair that could be spun into warm clothing. The brilliant white coat of this Spitz breed is set off by the dog's dark eyes and smiling black lips. Like most Spitz breeds, they are bold dogs but inclined to be noisy. **Right:** The Dalmatian is a breed whose spots should be round, well defined and distributed as evenly as possible over the body. Surprisingly the puppies are born white and the spots do nor appear until they are a few weeks old.

Above: This champion West Highland White Terrier is surrounded by some of the magnificent trophies it has won. The cheeky expression of these lively little terriers has made them very popular as pets. **Left:** There are six varieties of Dachshund. The smooth, the long-haired and the wire-haired types each come in standard and miniature sizes. All have the same sporting background, the miniatures, like this smooth red, being developed in Germany for rabbit hunting. **Far left:** Toy dogs like this Yorkshire Terrier are usually examined on a table by the judge at a show. Much patient training is needed for them to show themselves to the best advantage. Expert coat care in a breed like this plays an important part in the success of the exhibit. **Overleaf top:** These toy Poodles are the smallest of the three varieties in this breed. Their coats are clipped in the lion trim which is considered a necessity for the show ring. Though Poodles come in a number of colours, the blacks and the whites remain the most popular. **Overleaf bottom:** This ring full of Basset Hound exhibitors find it easier to position their dogs correctly if they get down on their knees.

In the field

It was as hunters that the dog and man were first associated and hunting dogs of one kind or another account for the greater number of breeds among modern dogs, even though they may not be put to such work today. Indeed the hunting instinct in the domesticated dog is probably stronger than that of the dog living in the wild, for the wild dog kills only what he needs to eat whereas the hunting instinct has been deliberately increased in the domestic dog and he will go on killing purely for its own sake.

Different types of dog have been developed for different roles, to hunt different kinds of prey and by different means. Some dogs are required to find the prey for others to kill, others to track it down and fight it to the death, some to force a way into its burrow or den and others to chase after the fleetest animals. The hounds, the terriers, the spaniels, the retrievers and the pointers, even when kept today as pets or in a miniaturized 'toy' form carry the character of their original type.

The hounds can be divided into two distinct groups: those that hunt by scent and those that hunt by sight. The gazehounds, those that hunt by sight, were not the earliest form of dog but records of them go back in history further than any other type of breed because they were a popular feature of ancient Egyptian life, appearing in hunting scenes from over 4,000 years ago. Gazehounds were bred to hunt a wide variety of quarry in open country where it could easily be seen. They were unleashed when quarry was in sight and streaked off after it. Speed and determination were the first priorities in their makeup. Stamina was necessary too, but less necessary in a fast dog that could catch a hare over a short distance than in a slower dog which would have to pursue it farther before gaining ground.

By the time of Christ interest in the Greyhound, perhaps the most familiar of all the gazehounds, had already changed from thinking of it as an animal to help catch food to an interest in the quality of the animal itself: the killing of the prey became less important than testing the speed and skill of one dog against another.

Keeping gazehounds became quite a status symbol and coursing hares was a popular sport among the nobility and one on which Queen Elizabeth I was very keen. During the nineteenth century attempts were made to popularize coursing in enclosed grounds. The hare was released at the end of a long enclosure which had an escape hole at the opposite end. This provided a test of speed: the dogs had to catch the hare before it reached the other end or escaped, but if they turned the hare before it reached the hole it would be finished. This method never became popular in England, although it is still used in Ireland, and it is now against the rules of the National Coursing Club. It is illegal in Britain to offer any captive wild animal to dogs for them to chase or kill.

Modern coursing in Spain, Britain, Australia and some other Commonwealth countries consists of two dogs at a time competing against each other in a series of heats. The dogs are put into special collars, linked by a long lead incorporating a mechanical release, which are known as slips. When a handle is pulled both dogs are released simultaneously and the collars fall to the ground. The 'slipper', a highly skilled expert, takes the two competing dogs and walks with them slightly ahead of the 'field' (spectators), which stretches out in a straight line on either side of him. When a hare gets up, the slipper hangs on to the dogs (by now going mad with excitement) until the hare has had sufficient 'lay', or start. The hare needs about 75 m (82 yds) start to give it time to get into its stride before the dogs are released. It is here that the slipper's expertize comes in; two young dogs would never catch up with a strong hare if it had that much start, but on the other hand two experienced dogs would kill a weaker hare without any chance to test their real ability. The judge follows behind the dogs mounted on horseback.

The first recorded Greyhound race using an artificial hare was held in Britain in 1867, in a field at Hendon, north of London. Surprisingly enough, it did not catch on, although the inaugural meeting appears to have been popular and well-attended. In 1890 the Americans made another attempt to popularize the idea, on the horse-race track at Miami. Again it failed

Above: The Lurcher is known as the gypsy's dog. It is usually a cross-bred greyhound type used for catching rabbits for the pot.
Opposite: The russet gold Hungarian Vizsla is an all-purpose gundog.

to receive support and it was not until 1909 that the first successful track opened at Tucson, Arizona. In 1926 an American, Charles Mann, successfully introduced the new sport to Britain and the first track was opened at Belle Vue, Manchester.

Since then Greyhound racing has become a very popular sport on both sides of the Atlantic and in Australia, attracting vast crowds, and huge sums of money change hands in the betting that takes place at the track. Because of this attempts to dope dogs, or to enter runners under a different identity, have frequently occurred and the sport is now rigidly controlled, with inspectors and veterinary officials on duty at every meeting to prevent frauds and unfair dealing.

Whippets, very like Greyhounds but somewhat smaller, were also used for coursing hares and rabbits and for racing in northern and midland England. A century ago they were the dogs of hard-working miners, and scarcely known elsewhere, but today they are popular show dogs. At the other extreme were the Borzois, the dogs of the Russian aristocracy, and the

Salukis, the pride of Arabian sheiks, who used them to hunt gazelle. The sheik and his retinue rode on Arab stallions and the servants walked with the hounds. Falcons were often used to locate the gazelle, although they could not kill it. When the falcon could be seen hovering above its quarry, the Salukis would be released. Even today's Salukis, generations removed from desert stock, will spot a bird (or a plane) in the sky long before it is visible to human eyes.

Whether the breed of prince or peasant, all gazehounds have the same elegant conformation, built for speed. The other hounds, the scent hounds, are much more varied in their appearance but are all much closer to the ground than their keen-sighted relations and share one very positive quality – staying power and stamina. Whereas the gazehound runs mute, and gives up when the quarry is out of sight, the

scent hound steadfastly follows the scent of its quarry and wears it down by its persistence. Scent hounds give voice when hunting, their cry indicating to the huntsmen who follow them not only the nature of the quarry but also its direction. They usually hunt in packs, but the pack leader is now the huntsman.

At first big, strong hounds were in favour and, as they often hunted in thick forest, the ability to stick to a line was more important than speed. As the great forests were felled to clear more agricultural land, a lighter, faster hound was gradually produced. Today the typical hunting prey is not the noble stag or the wild boar but the fox – although it was not until the mid-eighteenth century that foxhunting became a popular sport. Earlier countrymen thought of the fox as vermin, to be killed in any way possible.

The records of some foxhound packs go back to the early eighteenth century, and the Master of Foxhounds Association in Britain has kept a stud book since 1880. Nevertheless hounds from different packs vary considerably, having been developed to suit their own particular territory.

The English Foxhound is the main foxhound type, both in its name country and in Scotland and Ireland, but there is a Welsh Foxhound that appears to be older. The rough-coated Welsh Foxhound is claimed to be descended from the original hounds of Gaul. Foxhounds in America, New Zealand and Australia are descended from English stock and look very like English Foxhounds but in America there are also American Foxhounds which are a quite separate strain developed to suit the country in which they hunt.

The Beagle, which looks rather like a small foxhound, is a much older type of dog which was probably used for hunting hares by the ancient Greeks. Beagles are usually followed by huntsmen on foot, not by riders, and there is much less show about beagling than with foxhunting. The beagler's interest is in watching the hounds working and hunt followers must be very fit and very keen for they may have to run across bogs and moors in all kinds of weather.

In Canada and America the Beagle has become even more popular than in its native country, and the

Left: Labradors like these are expected to find and retrieve dead and wounded birds for the sportsman. They are expected to be 'soft-mouthed' and carry the bird without marking it.
Above: A pack of Bloodhounds is a very rare sight. These are following a drag, i.e. an artificially laid scent.

American Kennel Club registers more than 60,000 of the breed each year. Sometimes they hunt in packs to run down their quarry, the cottontail rabbit, but they are used more extensively in conjunction with guns, when their job is to push the rabbit out into the open. Their good voices enable the hunters to know when they pick up a trail, and whether the quarry is approaching or going away. In England small packs of Beagles are also sometimes used in the same way.

The Basset was used centuries ago on the Continent to hunt boar, deer and wolves but did not appear in Britain until the mid-nineteenth century. Bassets too are now used for hunting hare but have never become as popular as the Beagle. This is probably because they are much more independent dogs and do not hunt so well as a pack. Nevertheless, they are terrific hunters

and the music of a pack of Bassets in full cry is worth going a long way to hear. In America and in Europe the Basset is used more as a gun dog, to find and push game out of thick cover.

There are probably about 90 different types of scent hound recognized around the world, often named for their region or for the game they hunt, or used to hunt: the Staghound, Otterhound, Coonhound (developed in America to hunt the raccoon), Harrier and the Dachshund (which means 'badger dog' in German). The Bloodhound, the closest survivor of the hunting dogs of the Middle Ages, was originally used to hunt deer and boar and retains the excellent 'voice' of the ancient St Hubert Hound, but it was also discovered to have an extraordinary ability to track human beings. There are many records of Bloodhounds being used (often successfully) in the days of Border fighting between Scotland and England. Today the breed is used, usually singly and on a tracking line, almost exclusively to track people, although Bloodhounds are sometimes also hunted in packs with mounted followers. They are used by prison authorities in many parts of the world, their

task being to track down escaped criminals. Contrary to common belief, Bloodhounds do not attack their quarry and indeed usually greet him like a long-lost friend, slobbering all over him. This is why they are usually hunted on a tracking line enabling their handler to keep up with them. Once on the track, the dog must ignore all other tracks, human or animal. Here the Bloodhound has no equal, and it is not uncommon for one to pick up a track several days old and stick to it, even when it has been crossed by several fresh tracks.

It is not only the hounds which hunt the fox, for the Fox Terriers have a long-earned right to their name. Although between the World Wars they were more popular as pets and show dogs, they have long been used in association with hounds or on their own to creep underground in pursuit of foxes and badgers, to bolt foxes and rabbits and to kill rats. Today many of the terrier breeds seem far removed from the image of the tough working dog, but even the diminutive Yorkshire Terrier, with its glamorous long silky coat, would recognize its larger predecessor which was once kept on farms all over the Yorkshire moors and dales to exterminate the rats.

The name terrier comes from the Latin *terra*, meaning ground, and all terriers except the Boston Terrier, which does not belong in the terrier group at all, were bred for the same job. A terrier, like a hound, needs a good voice to keep in touch with the huntsmen with which he is working. Once a terrier has marked

Above: The terrier's job is to go to ground after vermin and these Norfolk Terriers are doing just that. **Top right**: The smooth Fox Terrier should be built like a cleverly made Hunter, giving the impression of speed and endurance. **Bottom right**: Border Terriers are workmanlike animals, big enough to keep up with the hounds and compact enough to bolt hillside foxes from their homes. **Overleaf left**: The Australian Terrier is one of the few terrier breeds that are not of British origin. **Overleaf right**: The Airedale is nicknamed the 'King of Terriers' as it is the largest in this group. Airedales are used as police dogs on the Continent.

its quarry underground, he should keep on barking to let the men on the surface know his whereabouts. They can then dig down and come to grips with the fox or badger. A silent dog can easily be lost or injured underground and never heard of again. The tendency of many of the smaller terriers to enjoy the sound of their own voices is, however, not always appreciated by owners today, who no longer want to work them.

Many of the rough-haired breeds which have become popular as pets require careful grooming and special cuts and trims have become customary for them. However, even the dog that visits the beauty parlour will probably still retain much of his fighting character and require firm handling. His qualities will make him an excellent guard dog and a loyal companion, whether he be Welsh, Irish, Australian, Norfolk, Bedlington, Airedale, Staffordshire, one of the several

Scottish Terriers or any of the numerous other terrier breeds that are known today.

Dogs can hunt for game in cover that no man could penetrate and they can catch the scent of prey which men could never find, but the falconer or bowman of the past (and the sportsman with a gun of more recent times) wanted to exercise their skill in the actual kill. Dogs were developed which would find and flush out game but in which the instinct to chase and catch were restrained to match the sportsman's needs. Yet such self-control – enabling a dog to stop in his tracks and watch another gain his prize – had to be coupled with a tremendous enthusiasm to hunt, demanding a very careful balance between the submissive and the hunting instincts.

Early references to game dogs such as these call them all spaniels and it is often said that the first spaniels came from Spain. Whether it is true or not there is a legend about how they got their name. In ancient times when the Carthaginians landed in Spain, the first thing they saw were hundreds of rabbits scurrying from bush to bush. So the soldiers all shouted 'span, span' which in their language meant 'rabbit'. The country was consequently named Hispania, or Rabbitland, and the dogs used for hunting the rabbits were called spaniels.

Even though they were all known as spaniels, these dogs had different functions. Springing spaniels found birds like partridge and quail and flushed them into nets. Setting spaniels or 'couchers' also used their noses to find coveys but, instead of flushing the birds, they showed they had found game by freezing into position with head held low, one forefoot raised and tail rigidly held out behind. The aim was to pin the birds to the ground long enough for a moveable net to be drawn over both birds and dog. The working of these springing spaniels foreshadows that of modern spaniel breeds and that of the setting spaniels, our setters and pointers.

When the development of quicker loading and more accurate firearms made it possible to shoot flying birds at a distance, it became the role of the flushing spaniel to put up the birds for the guns, rather than for the falcon, or to drive the birds or rabbits into nets. The dead or wounded bird now fell some distance from the sportsman, and often in places difficult to reach, so dogs were given another role to learn: finding the shot game and bringing it back.

When a wild dog has caught its prey, it will often carry it in its mouth to its den or to some other safe hideaway to eat in peace, and this behaviour pattern forms the basis for the retrieving instinct which has been carefully nurtured in the gundog breeds. Retrievers must learn to carry birds and other game very gently in their mouths so that it is not damaged by their teeth, yet grip it firmly enough not to drop it. They must be prepared to bring it back from wherever it falls, and some breeds with oily and water-resistant coats have been developed for water work.

Top left: The wire Fox Terrier should have a coat with the texture of coconut matting. Few are used for their original job of bolting foxes but they are popular pets.
Bottom left: The wistful look of this Skye Terrier gives little indication of the breed's gameness or its punishing strength of jaw. The dog is one of a number of short-legged terriers from Scotland, all of which were bred to go to ground. The modern Skye still has the courage of its ancestors but is hampered by an extremely long coat. **Above:** The Clumber Spaniel is a rare breed and the heavyweight among the spaniels.

Top left: One of the more curious and inexplicable inherited behaviour patterns is the attitude adopted by bird dogs like this Pointer when they catch the scent of a game bird. The rigid pose is often maintained for quite a long period of time.

Bottom left: The Soft-Coated Wheaten Terrier is a tough, hardy Irish breed which has just begun to make headway in the show ring.
Above: The Cairn Terrier is one of the most popular of pets with a shaggy, unkempt charm all its own.

Some modern breeds, especially the European gundogs, have been developed as all-round pointer/retrievers and will tackle most of the jobs involved in the course of a shoot, but traditionally retrievers and spaniels are expected to work on all game birds, wildfowl, rabbits and hares once they are fully experienced, while pointers and setters (known as bird-dogs) perform completely different work. Pointers and setters are traditionally only concerned with the unshot bird – their job is to range far and wide in great sweeps, known as 'quartering' the ground. By nose alone they locate the distant birds, immediately freezing to a point which they maintain until the sportsman comes up to them. Both man and

Above: The Chesapeake Bay Retriever is an American gundog, a specialist in retrieving wildfowl and working in the toughest of cold and wet conditions. The coat is very oily and almost totally water-resistant, and the dogs are a faded tan or dead-grass colour. **Right:** The Field Spaniel was a popular dog at the beginning of this century but is now only kept by a handful of enthusiasts.

dog then move slowly towards the birds until they flush and fly away. The shot is fired and, whether hit or miss, the dog must drop to the ground and remain there until led away to start a fresh beat.

Whistle and hand signals are often used to ensure that the dog does not miss any ground when

quartering, or to 'drop' a particular area.

There is a wide range of gundog breeds from which to choose. For one or two sportsmen engaged in rough shooting the best choice is probably a spaniel, such as the large, versatile English Springer. But members of a syndicate, where beaters are employed to drive the game, might well prefer retrievers.

Many sportsmen send their dogs to professional trainers to be taught their jobs, but there is no reason why anyone with some knowledge of dogs and shooting should not train their own – and some parts of the training will help to make even a pet dog's life more interesting. Indeed, there is nothing more satisfying than working closely with an intelligent, co-operative dog that you have trained yourself. Training starts as soon as you acquire the dog, from the moment that you first put him in his bed and make him stay there. You must get the puppy settled, confident and at home with you, then you can teach such early commands as sit, stay, heel, not to jump up and to come when called. He must learn and obey that important word 'No'. When he knows all these lessons, and his second teeth are fully through the gums, you can begin to turn him into a useful worker.

To teach retrieving, make a small, sausage-shaped dummy from a woollen stocking stuffed with straw and newspaper. Buy a new washing line made of plaited cord from which to cut a length for the dog to wear in training in place of his collar and lead. Make a running noose at one end with a knot to prevent it drawing too tight and choking the dog. At the other end make a knot to stop the cord unravelling or slipping through your fingers. You may be able to buy both dummy and cord ready prepared. Put on the cord and make your dog sit on your left side. Take the dummy and waggle it in front of his nose so that he tries to get it. Then throw the dummy on to open ground in his full view. As he rushes after it drop the cord, turn and *run* back towards his *closed* kennel door, or the back door if his bed is in the house. He will instinctively run after you, whereupon intercept him, take the dummy from him gently without pulling and make much of him. He must be made to realize that he has done something extremely clever and that you are pleased both with him and the dummy. If he gets past you shut his door and get the dummy from him there, praising him in the same way. Repeat this exercise once more and finish his lesson for the day.

From now on, for the rest of his life, he must always be made to sit, for a few seconds at least, before being allowed to go for the dummy. Always send him with the command 'Hie lost' and a forward wave of the hand. Never alter a word of command once taught.

As he progresses vary this lesson by throwing two dummies, one to right and one to left, keeping him sitting. Then with the usual command and wave of the hand towards the dummy you want him to pick, send him to retrieve. Either pick up the second dummy yourself or make him pick up both in the order you require. He must not be allowed to anticipate your wishes but must obey your hand signals. Occasionally keep him sitting for a minute or so to develop his memory and marking ability, forcing him to note the exact fall and remember the spot accurately. Then he must learn to find an hidden dummy by his nose as well as from your signals. This unseen dummy may puzzle him at first, but if you use hand signals and his usual command he will soon learn that he is being sent for something that he has not seen fall.

It is necessary to teach all breeds of gundog to understand and obey whistle signals. This is done by going through the basic lessons giving the usual signals by raised hand and directional waves but substituting whistles for commands.

To teach the dog to retrieve from water you need a non-sinkable dummy. Make him sit and then throw the dummy so that it floats just within his depth. Let him get it. Next time throw it a few feet further out so that he just becomes waterborne as he teeters to reach it. The following stage is to throw it just out of his depth so that he has to swim those important few strokes to it and back to the shore. After this he will swim any distance, as he gains confidence that he can swim. At all times, on land or in water, he must come right up and place the dummy tenderly and willingly into your outstretched hand.

Getting a dog used to gunfire requires two people,

one to fire the gun and the other – you – to give him his usual 'seen' retrieve. On no account use a rifle. Take a shotgun or a quiet cap pistol, as the sound must not be a sharp loud crack. The 'gun' stands downwind of the dog about 45 m (50 yd) away. Throw the dummy so that the dog sees it fall. After a few seconds at the 'sit' send him to retrieve. Just as he is reaching out to pick the dummy up the shot is fired. He may hesitate but encourage him to complete the retrieve, then make a great fuss of him. If he is really nervous, increase the distance between puppy and gun.

Once free from gunshyness and good at all his lessons, transfer the dog from dummy to game by fastening a hen pheasant's wing on to his dummy by strong elastic bands. Once used to that, get hold of a cold but fresh bird or three-quarters grown rabbit to substitute for his winged dummy, thus completing his transfer from dummies to real game. He should now be ready for an easy day in the shooting field and will gain his further experience there.

Working with pointers and setters is highly specialized and if possible you should already be experienced at working bird dogs before embarking on training your puppy. Then you will know what you are doing, which is vital when so much depends on the handler.

The attractive appearance and excellent temperament of the gundog breeds make many people, who would never dream of going out hunting, want to own them as pets, and many others are raised as show dogs rather than working dogs. Generations of careful breeding for kindness and obedience, willingness and intelligence have produced qualities ideal for the family dog or the gundog. Nevertheless there is a difference in some breeds between the working and the showbred dog, although before becoming a show champion a gundog must pass certain tests under qualified experts. Retrievers and spaniels must show that they will hunt and retrieve tenderly (and spaniels must face covert). Pointers and setters must show that they have the instinct to hunt and point. All gundogs must show that they are not gunshy, even when off the lead. At the same time it must be remembered that gundogs have been carefully selected for their natural interest in birds and animals. Unless they are given the proper training they will manifest these instincts in an interest in sheep, deer and poultry. Even a dog that has never seen a gun will have considerable energy, needing space to live and adequate exercise, and the big gundogs should not be chosen for life in a small city apartment.

Right: A yellow Labrador walks obediently to heel. Should the gun be fired the dog will immediately sit and wait until it is sent to retrieve the fallen bird. Yellow Labradors are more popular as pets but most shooting men prefer the black colour for work in the field.

Left: The Continental gundog breeds are expected to find, flush and retrieve game when it has been shot. This large Munsterlander is completing a retrieve which obviously started with the dead bird falling into water. **Above:** Racing greyhounds travel at more than 50 k/h (30 mph) and injuries to their legs and feet are a common hazard.

Overleaf: Hound trailing is a sport confined to the north of England. Betting is heavy on the outcome of each race and the followers of the sport tend to be fanatical in their devotion. Trail hounds look like racily built foxhounds and follow an aniseed and paraffin 'drag' laid over ten miles of punishing Fell country, a race which may take up to 45 minutes.

Above: A pack of Beagles set out for a day's hunting. They hunt the hare and are followed on foot, providing an energetic and exciting day's sport. **Top left:** The Irish Terrier is sometimes nicknamed the 'Red Devil' as it tends to have rather a cavalier attitude to other dogs. **Bottom left:** Working Setters like this one tend to differ markedly from the more glamorous exhibition type. Few show dogs work successfully in the field.

Overleaf: Harriers, midway in size between Beagles and Foxhounds, are an ancient breed which is becoming much rarer. Packs are used for hunting hares and are followed on horseback. Dogs like these, which have always been used to pack life, are totally unsuitable as pets. Their hunting instinct is too strong, and their energy and stamina too great, for them to settle into the less demanding life of a pet dog.

Left: The Sealyham Terrier was created in the nineteenth century by a Welsh sportsman, Captain Edwardes, who wanted a fearless, short-legged terrier prepared to tackle anything from polecats to badgers. His young dogs were tested for courage and those that did not come up to his requirements were summarily shot. The modern Sealyham is rather a comic character with plenty of personality.

Above: All dogs can swim naturally but not all take to the water as readily as the retriever breeds. This working-type Golden Retriever is fetching a wounded duck. Note how gently the dog is carrying the struggling bird.

Overleaf left: Basset Hound packs are not all that common, for the breed is now better known as a pet and showdog. The working hound tends to be less cumbersome in build. Bassets hunt the hare and are followed on foot. To the lovers of hound music the baying of Bassets on a scent is one of the most exciting of sounds.

Overleaf right: Few purebred Otterhounds are left but this Scottish pack consists entirely of the old rough-coated type. Since water is a notoriously bad scenting medium, Otterhounds must have exceptionally good noses to be able to follow their quarry. The outlook for Otterhounds seems bleak as public opinion is against otter hunting. The otter is now an endangered species and hunting it is the only reason for the breed's existence.

Left: The English Springer Spaniel is a popular gundog with the rough-shooting man. It is big and robust enough to tackle anything that is likely to be found during a day's shooting. A breed like this must find and flush the game as well as retrieving it when it has been shot. Springers are also popular show and pet dogs.
Below: The Irish Water Spaniel, as the name suggests, is a gundog for those interested in wildfowling. The coat of tight, oily ringlets enables the dog to work in cold, wet conditions without discomfort. Like some of the other Irish breeds, the Water Spaniel can be a bit of a clown. When its interest is caught it can be a brilliant worker but it does tend to be temperamental. **Right:** Man is a hunting animal, with his dog as an enthusiastic assistant. This group are rabbit hunting.

Right: The Sussex Spaniel was a well-known sporting dog in the nineteenth century and is a very handsome dog with a rich golden liver coat. It is a slow worker and credited with the greatest determination in pushing out both fur and feather from the thickest of coverts. It was especially good in the gorse thickets of its native county. Times and the fashion in gundogs have changed, however, and the Sussex Spaniel's habit of giving tongue whilst working does not suit the modern sportsman. Consequently the breed has lost a lot of support and is struggling to survive.

Below: The German Weimaraner is one of the dual-purpose Continental gundogs which will both point and retrieve. The silver-grey colouring is unique and it has been given the nickname of the 'grey ghost'. The breed was established in the nineteenth century by a group of German sportsmen who were interested in a dog of all-round ability. A breed club was established and kept very close control over all litters bred. Dogs which were considered temperamentally or physically sub-standard were destroyed. Consequently the breed did not become established outside Germany until some thirty years ago.

What makes a champion?

In 1835 the British Parliament passed a law which put an end to bull baiting, rat pits and organized dog fights, in which 'entertainments' men had tested the skill and courage of their dogs against each other. Their abolition left a void among those to whom the sport had given pleasure, an opportunity for betting and a source of pride in their dogs. Instead men began to match their dogs against each other on appearance only. Gradually, unofficial standards began to be accepted and primitive dog shows began to be held in taverns patronised by the sporting fraternity. Such functions ultimately attracted the attention of a different kind of dog owner. The first organized dog show in the modern sense took place at Newcastle-upon-Tyne, in northern England, in 1859, with two classes in which dogs could be entered: pointers and setters.

The development of railways, linking different regions and speeding transportation, made it possible for dogs to be entered in competitions up and down the country (and there are tales of a dog being entered under one name and record in one town and quite a different one in another) so that varieties and strains which had previously been known in a very limited locality attracted attention over a wide area. Dogs were frequently sent to shows unaccompanied and the conditions provided for them were often far from good. In 1873 a group of dog enthusiasts, under the patronage of the Prince of Wales, formed the first British Kennel Club with the aim of changing this. Two months after its foundation the Club held its first show which proved a tremendous success, and the Kennel Club has been recognized as the ruling show body in Britain ever since. As well as organizing shows, it produced a stud book – the first appeared in 1874 – which every year since then has been the record against which the breeding and achievement of every dog qualified for entry in a British show can be checked.

Over 3,500 shows are held under Kennel Club rules every year in Britain, as well as about 300 field and working trials. All dogs shown at recognized shows, which means practically all dog shows in Britain, must be registered at the Kennel Club, and the same applied to field trials for gundogs, working trials for police dogs and obedience classes. It does not, however, apply to sheepdog trials, which are held under the rules of the International Sheepdog Society; hound shows, which are run by the Masters of Foxhounds Association; and coursing matches, which are held under the rules of the National Coursing Club.

As the cult of showing dogs has spread throughout the world, governing bodies have been founded in each country to see fair play. The American Kennel Club was organized in 1884 and a European body, the Fedération Cynologique Internationale, in which a number of countries participate, was set up in 1911. Anyone contemplating showing a dog should contact their own Kennel Club to find out what shows are available and what rules and regulations must be adhered to.

Dog shows are beauty competitions where the construction, shape and movement of one animal is compared with another, and both are measured against the breed standard, a portrait in words of what the ideal dog of that breed should look like. Every breed that is shown has its own standard, a description that was originally written or approved by the parent club which looks after that particular breed's interests. This description was then approved by and lodged with the national Kennel Club, which reserves the right to restrict its reproduction. Breed standards vary in their quality according to the ability of the people who wrote them, and a written description is open to a number of interpretations. These two factors give dog showing the fascination of unpredictability because if everyone agreed as to which was the best dog, showing would stop. As it is, the really great dogs in each breed are generally recognized by judges and win fairly consistently. Other dogs will have a more chequered career, winning one day under a judge who likes their type and being ignored another day by a judge who is impressed by something rather different. Really poor breed specimens will not win anywhere and eventually are withdrawn from showing.

Left: The American Cocker Spaniel was for many years top dog in the States and is now firmly established in Britain. It has a more domed head than the English Cocker and a heavier coat. **Above:** The coat of the Yorkshire Terrier needs expert care but the dogs seem to enjoy the fuss.

It is difficult to explain the attraction of showing animals to those who do not share it. It is certainly not done for the cash value of the prizes, and very few people have ever made money by showing dogs. A lot of satisfaction is to be derived from producing an animal to such a high standard that it beats all the others in its class. To win best of breed or, better still, best in show at a championship show is a very real thrill and one experienced by comparatively few people. To those interested in genetics, the breeding of any animal to certain high standards of perfection is a never-ending source of pleasure and satisfaction.

What do dog shows accomplish? They have now been in existence for well over 100 years, during which time they have steadily increased in popularity. Looking back over that span of time one can see that the appearance of many breeds has been greatly improved and that all breeds are much more standardized and uniform. Public interest in pedigree livestock has grown tremendously and the show ring provides the publicity that each breed requires if it is to survive. This factor is very important, as every dog breeder depends on the sale of surplus puppies to the public as pets. Nearly every breed was originally

created to do a specific job of work. As mechanization and urbanization removed the need for dogs to take cattle to market, or turn spits, or pull carts, the kinds of dogs that did these jobs tended to die out. The number of extinct breeds is quite a long one, but many others were saved from disappearing by the interest of show exhibitors.

What the show ring cannot do is measure a dog's working ability. The winner of a beauty contest may take your eye but you cannot tell what she would be like to live with, and the same thing applies to a winning dog. One can assume that the temperament of a winner is sound. After all, it has just been examined intimately by the judge, who is probably a total stranger, and it has shown neither fear nor aggression. As it has won, one can assume that the dog is constructed soundly enough to do its original job of work. What one cannot assume is that the dog

Above: The Scottish Terrier trimmed like this one for the show ring presents a very different picture from one left in the rough. Clever trimming can help to hide a dog's faults.
Right: A ring full of Bedlington Terriers are lined up for the judge's final inspection. Trimming with scissors and razor emphasizes the curves.

has the ability, the drive or the brains for its original job. How much this matters depends on your point of view. Those who want working gundogs or working sheepdogs buy them from working stock rather than show stock. Many working dogs are not suitable as pets, having tremendous energy and a compulsion to work which need to be utilized if the animal is not to become neurotic and destructive. Most pet owners want a placid friendly animal and this temperament is equally necessary in a show dog.

A more serious criticism of the show ring is that in some breeds physical peculiarities have been exaggerated until they have become a hazard to the dog's health. The reasons for this can very often be found in a poorly worded breed standard. A description written 70 years ago saying that the nose should be as short as possible has led to a modern dog with breathing difficulties and a tendency to skin troubles in the deeply folded wrinkles on its face. Some body shapes predispose an animal to whelping difficulties or spinal trouble. These are some of the rather more insidious dangers that occur when dogs are bred solely for their looks.

To anyone with an inclination to take up pedigree dog breeding as a hobby or who feels like showing the dog they already have, the first advice is to go along to several shows and try to find out what it is all about. Go to one or two big championship shows, but also take a look at your local show because that is where you should start showing. Watch how the experts handle their dogs and don't forget that today's experts were yesterday's novices.

Obviously every exhibitor wants to breed and show a top dog, but even a top dog will not be a winner unless trained and presented to perfection. The bloom and sparkle of perfect health are necessities for success. Good movement in the show ring and grooming play their part, and some training for the show ring will help your dog to show himself to his best advantage. Presentation and showmanship will not turn a bad dog into a good one, but it can make him look a great deal better.

Show training must start long before the animal is entered for his first show. The show puppy should have daily lessons in standing and posing and must be taught to accept the sort of examination which the

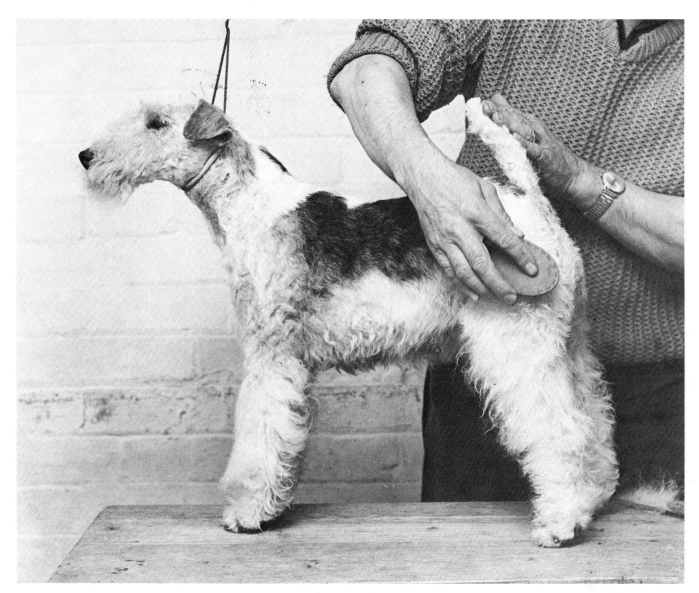

Left: The Gordon Setter needs little show preparation as its coat has the gleam of good health. **Above**: The wire Fox Terrier needs expert trimming and is often left to professional handlers. **Overleaf**: Judging the finished product.

judge will give, inspecting his mouth and running his hands over the dog's body to assess its construction.

Confidence on the part of the handler is also important, for any nervousness will be transferred to the dog. That is why a professional handler can often get better results with a dog he has never seen before than the owner, who knows the dog well. It is important that the dog is relaxed when he is with other dogs, so a puppy should be given plenty of opportunity to meet other dogs. Training classes can be a help and some canine societies run handling classes for 'beauty' dogs as opposed to 'obedience' dogs.

The dog's appearance depends a great deal on what has been done before the show. With so much difference between the various breeds, there must obviously be equally great differences in preparation. 'Breed books' devoted to each breed often give detailed advice on how to prepare that particular breed for the show ring, and experienced exhibitors are usually very pleased to help a novice. Nevertheless, there are several general points worth mentioning. No amount of grooming or trimming can make up for the lack of a first-class diet and carefully controlled exercise (a show dog does not have to be as fit as, say, a racing Greyhound and, in fact, should carry more flesh to give a more rounded appearance).

Many newcomers to dog showing are confused because the judge at one show will frequently place the same animals in a different order from the judge at another show. This is because each judge may interpret the written standard in his own way. One judge's idea of what is 'moderately wide between the ears' may be very different from another's. It is a good thing, maybe, that judges do differ; if everyone could agree on the perfect dog, then that dog would win all the prizes and there would be no point in anyone else entering their dogs in competitions.

The sick pet

Looking after your dog's well-being when it is sick is something you must share with your veterinary surgeon. He will only be able to see the physical symptoms in the dog and will rely upon you to tell him of changes in behaviour and symptoms that have passed or do not appear in a physical examination. Sometimes he will want to keep an animal under observation or take him in for treatment, but in most cases the psychological disturbance of being away from home and master make it preferable for treatment to be given at home. Your vet will give you specific instructions for any special nursing needs but everyone should learn how to give pills and medicines and how to cope with minor accidents and injuries, and with the emergency treatment that may save an animal's life before it can receive veterinary attention.

Sadly, traffic accidents are the most common accidents suffered by dogs. A dog that has been hit by a car is almost certainly suffering from shock – the first symptoms are paleness of the gums and an inability to move – and possibly from internal injuries and should therefore be moved as little as possible. However, shock reaction can lead to death in only a few hours and veterinary attention should be sought immediately. Police will help you find the nearest veterinary surgery or clinic.

If there is excessive bleeding it must be stopped. First check that there is nothing in the wound, then apply a pad of gauze if any is available (if not, use a clean handkerchief, torn sheet or the most suitable clean covering you can find). Then bandage firmly over the pad. If blood seeps through, rebandage on top and take the dog to the vet immediately. To move a large injured dog with as little disturbance as possible, it is best to use a blanket. Slide it gently under the dog and, with one person at each end holding two corners, gently lift the dog into a car.

If the dog is suffering from internal bleeding, his breathing will be rapid and shallow, his skin will feel clammy, his pulse will be rapid and he may be unconscious. In this case, simply get him to the veterinary surgeon just as fast as you can.

If the dog is conscious remember that he is frightened and likely to bite, so taping or tying a muzzle around his jaws may save you getting a nasty injury yourself.

To prevent accidents when you go out with your dog, you will obviously keep him on a leash until you are in a park or open country well away from traffic, but even in parks and in ponds and streams careless people often leave dangerous litter and it is easy for a dog to get a cut or scratch. This will probably not cause serious bleeding but even small cuts need washing and bandaging to keep dirt out so that they will not become infected. Small cuts on the ear, however, rarely stop bleeding by themselves and require careful treatment to avoid excessive loss of blood.

On the limbs deeper cuts with severe bleeding should be controlled by making a tourniquet – in an emergency a tie or a piece of soft cloth such as a handkerchief could be used – but no tourniquet should be left on longer than 20 minutes at a time. Get veterinary attention as soon as possible so that the wound can be properly cleaned out and dressed and antibiotic treatment given. Stitching might also be necessary in some cases.

If you suspect a dog to have a fractured bone in the leg it should be supported by a splint to prevent further damage as you take him to the vet, but for any other injury wrap the dog up in a blanket. In fact broken bones do not demand such immediate treatment as some other injuries. Any form of eye injury, however, should be treated immediately, even if bleeding does not occur. Wasp and bee stings are usually serious only when they occur in the mouth and the consequent swelling obstructs breathing.

Naturally, you will take care that all poisons are kept where the dog cannot get at them, but it is not possible to protect a dog from poisons outside the house. Vomiting is often the main symptom, followed by collapse in a few hours. Common rat poisons often produce bleeding of the gums and vomiting of blood. If you know a dog has eaten a poisonous substance force it to swallow a crystal of washing soda or a strong salt solution. If this is given within three hours

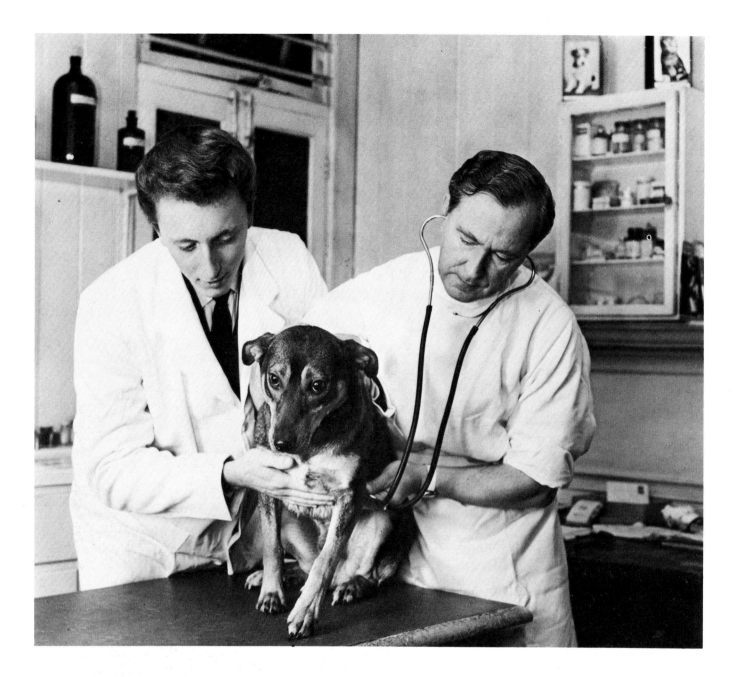

of eating the poison there will be a reasonable chance that the dog will vomit it back before it has been absorbed.

Vomiting may also be caused by an object lodged in the intestine: chicken and chop bones are particularly dangerous in this way and surgery is often necessary to remove them. Always treat vomiting as worthy of a vet's attention.

Small rubber balls are the most usual cause of choking in dogs. The dog will be in considerable distress and, although able to breathe, will be unable to swallow and will salivate profusely. You will probably be able to feel the ball in his throat. The dog should be seen as soon as possible by a veterinary surgeon, who may have to anaesthetize him before removing the object.

Dogs sometimes also get a rubber ball stuck behind their molar teeth, causing an obstruction. If possible

Above: A routine examination with a stethoscope. **Right**: Push a pill as far down the dog's throat as you can. Then hold his muzzle shut and gently stroke his throat until you feel the animal swallow. Some dogs can be bribed to take pills.

try to remove the ball, but be careful not to push it further down. Bones, pieces of stick and even stones can equally become lodged in the back of the mouth and cause a nasty wound. A dog with something wedged in his mouth usually paws frantically at his mouth or rubs it along the ground, slobbering profusely. Open his mouth carefully, taking care not to get bitten, and see if you can pull out the offending object. If you cannot get hold of it take the dog to the veterinary surgeon, who will give him an anaesthetic before removing the object and treating the wound.

Fleas, parasitic worms and ear mites are dealt with

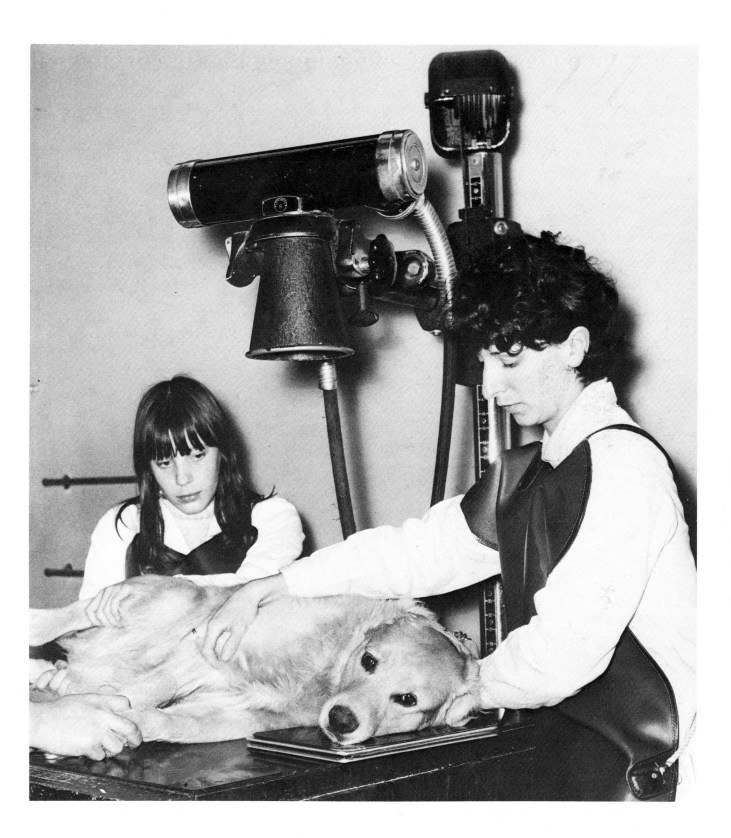

Left: This dog involved several men in a
hazardous rescue operation. No one is quite
sure how the animal reached the rocky ledge on
which it was found. However all ended safely,
the only injury being the dog's paws made sore
by its attempts to climb up the rocks.
Above: Modern X-ray techniques have been
the greatest help to veterinary surgeons.
Through its use, diagnosis can be more
accurate and treatment more specific.

under general care but small abrasions in the ear, caused by scratching or by a foreign object, such as a grass seed, can produce a bacterial infection, characterized by puss and a strong smell, which should be treated rapidly. Prolonged ear scratching can make the layers of the ear separate and fill with blood. This condition, called aural haematoma, looks like a swollen ear. An operation is usually necessary to cure it.

'Ringworm' is not a worm but a fungus which is first noticed as small bald patches, often in the shape of a ring (hence the common name). Such fungal conditions spread easily from one dog to another and may affect people, leaving scars on the skin. The dog should be treated as soon as the infection is discovered and your own doctor consulted regarding possible human infection.

Two of the most serious diseases which dogs can catch are distemper and viral hepatitis. Distemper is unfortunately common and usually fatal. It is often seen in young puppies, although all ages are susceptible. The first signs are a cough, vomiting, loss of appetite, diarrhoea and a yellow discharge from the eyes and the nose. As the disease progresses, twitches and fits develop. Although the disease lasts for weeks, immediate attention is necessary for any hope of recovery.

Viral hepatitis is a disease affecting the liver and can also be fatal if left untreated. It is not a very common condition. Often the only signs are weakness, lethargy and weight loss. The dog has a very high temperature and usually pants. Jaundice eventually develops.

Fortunately the most serious common diseases, including distemper, viral and a bacterial hepatitis and a bacterial kidney infection, can be prevented by vaccination. Normally two vaccinations are given, one at ten and the other at twelve weeks of age, although an earlier vaccination is possible.

Like any human patient the sick dog needs comfort, quiet and consideration. He will need reassurance and gentle handling but will not want to be pestered.

Temperature can be an important guide to the progress of an illness and an important symptom in confirming one, and an owner should learn how to take a dog's temperature. A snub-nosed thermometer should be used – not the brittle kind that are put into human mouths – and after being greased with Vaseline it should be inserted, very gently, into the dog's rectum. If the dog objects you may need someone to hold him while you do it. Hold the thermometer for the time needed to register the temperature and do not let it go – dogs have been known to draw them right inside if the hold is released! A dog's normal temperature is about 38°C (101°F), or a little below in larger breeds. A rise to 39°C (103°F) is significant and higher would suggest the vet is needed. A drop in temperature is even more serious. In smaller dogs 37.4°C (100°F) should be taken as a warning and lower than 37°C (99°F)

demands attention. A temperature below 36°C (97.5°F) suggests the battle is being lost. Temperature must be maintained by heating or hotwater bottles.

At some time or another you are bound to have to give a dog some medicine. If this is liquid you will find it easier to put it into a small bottle, or a syringe, rather than trying to tip it out of a spoon. Have the dog sitting when you administer a dose and, if possible, recruit a helper to hold him steady. Insert a finger between his lips on one side of his mouth and pull them slightly apart and outwards to form a pocket into which you can pour the medicine. Hold his head slightly back and pour in only a small quantity at a time, which he can swallow easily. Continue slowly until he has taken the complete dose. Keep his mouth shut all the time and gently massage his throat to make sure that all the medicine is swallowed.

You may also have to administer a pill or capsule. Some people try to give these in food but that way the dog might spit them out or not eat the whole dose, and some medicines cannot be given with food because of the reactions they cause. The best method is to place your hand over the dog's face and on either side press his lips over his top teeth, which will make him open his mouth. Tip his head slightly backwards, and with your other hand drop the pill or capsule right at the back of the tongue. Take your hand away quickly, close the dog's mouth and hold it shut, watching for him to swallow. If he seems to be holding the pill in his mouth massage his throat or gently close his nostrils for a few seconds.

Top right: Dogs which are given large biscuits to chew and big raw bones to gnaw are liable to have few teeth troubles until old age. When tartar forms it can be seen as a brown deposit. This tends to push back the gums and finally loosen the teeth. The big incisor teeth are usually the first to collect tartar at the base and this can be scraped off with a dental scaler.
Bottom right: It is a wasteful and messy process to try and give liquid medicine from a spoon. Instead put the liquid in a small bottle and pour it gently into the pouch of skin formed if you pull out the corner of the dog's lips.

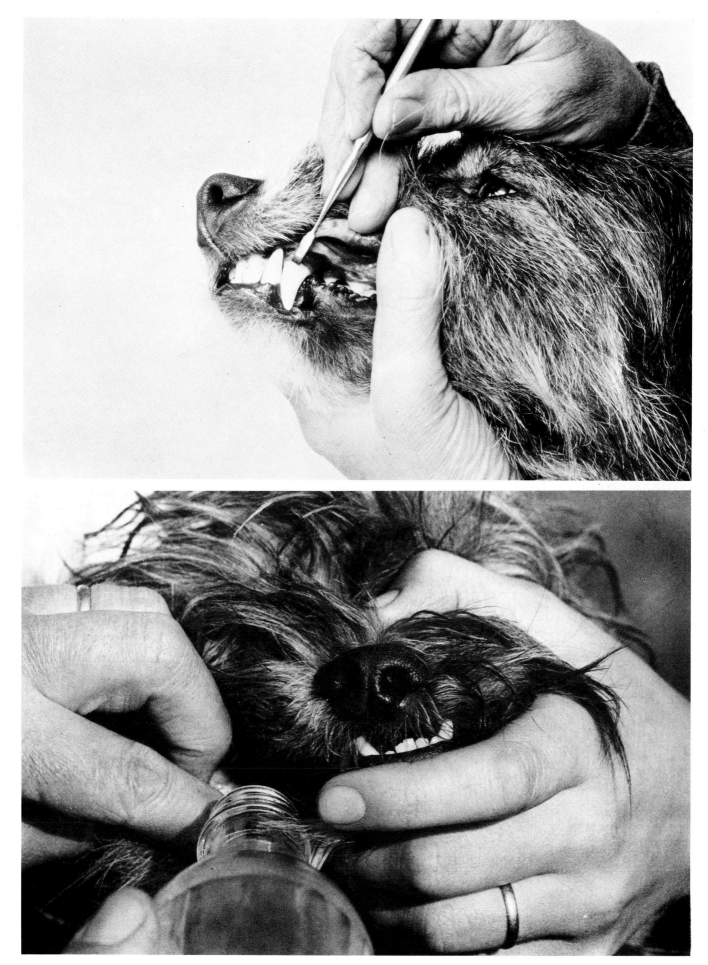

143

The world's favourite dogs

What puts a particular breed at the head of the popularity stakes? One might expect it to be its usefulness, obedience, friendly character and freedom from hereditary defect or disease. Certainly, without a plus rating for at least some of these qualities it is unlikely that many of the hundreds of dog breeds would have survived. However, at any given time, it is fashion rather than more practical reasons which often influences a dog's popularity.

It would seem natural that at the present time, when more people live in small city apartments, that the choice would fall upon the smaller, toy breeds which fit well in the restricted space of most modern homes, yet large dogs seem to be increasingly seen in city streets and parks, even if accommodation is restricted. While everyone talks of inflation and of having to economize, this does not seem to deter people from owning a dog which costs large sums to feed. Perhaps the popularity of Afghan Hounds and similar dogs today is a symbolic defiance of the restrictions of city life and the threat of economic crisis.

Indeed, the choice of dog does frequently seem to fulfil a psychological need, the animal bringing into its owner's life a grace and vitality that might otherwise be lacking. But sadly there are too many cases where a particular breed has been purchased as a status symbol, another commodity to be displayed to show the owner's wealth and position, or to act as a foil to a life style.

Often the owning of a particular type of dog by someone of position, or in the public eye, will draw attention to a breed of which, until then, many people were unaware. As well as having the cachet of being a dog selected by a leader of current taste, the breed will also have the exposure, perhaps before denied it, which enables it to be seen for its own virtues too. The nobility of past centuries may have boasted of the quality of their hounds, but lapdogs also won their place among the courtiers and their ladies. When newspapers, movies and the electronic media brought the world to everyman's breakfast table a photograph of a particular breed, its appearance in a television commercial, its choice by royalty or by a well-publicized movie star might take a dog from comparative oblivion to being a much sought-after breed.

In the 1930s the purchase of a Corgi by the then Duke of York for his daughter, the future Elizabeth II of England, did as much to popularize that breed as Queen Victoria's interest in the Collie – a breed which gained an ever greater world-wide popularity from the series of successful *Lassie* films made for cinema and television. A Walt Disney cartoon, based on a book by Dodie Smith, made many people want to own one of the dogs that featured in *A Hundred and One Dalmatians*. A whisky advertisement helped boost the fame of the Scottish Terrier and a paint commercial made many people want to own an Old English Sheepdog.

There are dangers here, for the demand for a particular type of dog can lead the less scrupulous breeders to offer defective puppies for sale and to breed from stock that are not of an acceptable standard, with the risk of lowering the general quality of the breed and of its temperament.

Some dog owners will always want to keep the tried and trusted breeds, while others will look for the exotic and always want something new. The days of creating brand new breeds have, however, almost certainly passed for the Kennel Clubs of the world now require very stringent conditions to be met before they will recognize a new breed. The unusual today is usually a breed already well established elsewhere.

The following are the breeds that currently head the charts in Britain and America: German Shepherd Dog (Alsatian), Doberman Pinscher, Irish Setter, Beagle, Smooth-haired Dachshund, St Bernard, Labrador Retriever, Yorkshire Terrier, American Cocker Spaniel, Miniature Schnauzer.

No doubt some of them will lose their places in the years to come, and be replaced by others, but the qualities which make certain breeds – it is up to you to decide which – such excellent pets and attractive dogs will ensure that they remain popular despite the fluctuating whims of fashion.

Previous page: The British Bulldog is an affectionate and loving beast despite his scowling expression.
Above: The Yorkshire Terrier makes a lively and intelligent companion. The pet Yorkie usually carries much less coat than its show counterpart and reveals itself as a true terrier in miniature. They are small enough to be tucked under the arm and yet strong and active enough to enjoy a walk with their owners.

Right: The handsome Irish Setter is a racy dog needing an active owner who has the time to provide enough exercise. They are such gay and happy dogs that they have always had plenty of admirers. The brilliance of their silky red coats is an added attraction. We are now so used to the chestnut colouring that they are often called Red Setters. However, in the early days of the breed, they were more often red and white and nineteenth-century portraits often show this type of colouring.

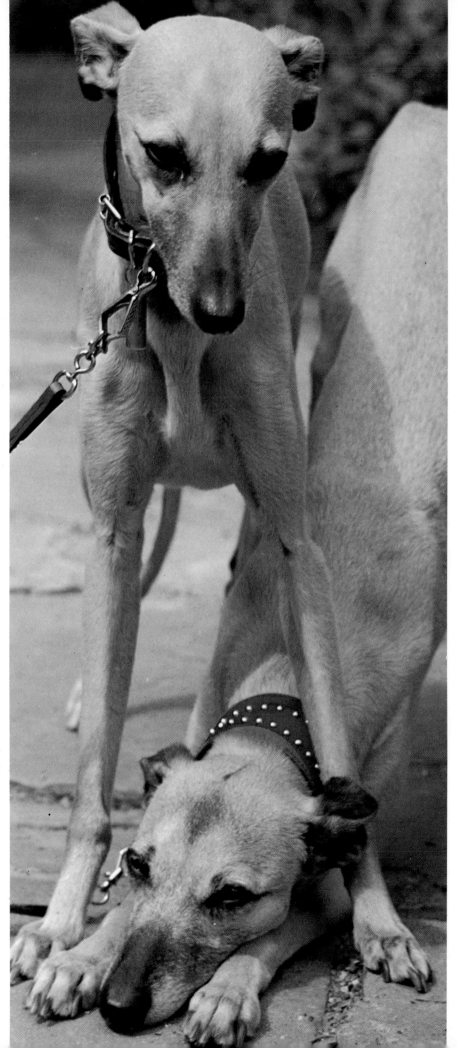

Right: The graceful Whippet is an ideal size for many modern homes. The smooth coat requires little in the way of attention and it is a gentle, affectionate breed.

Left: This Lhasa Apso puppy will have all the arrogant charm of the other Far Eastern breeds. They make good watchdogs and eye-catching pets, but this type of coat needs daily attention.

Overleaf left: The Pomeranian, like many toy dogs, is full of its own importance. Like all the Spitz breeds, of which this is a dwarf version, the Pomeranian likes the sound of its own voice.

Overleaf right: The drooping wrinkles of the Bloodhound give it a very dignified look. They tend to be gentle, rather sensitive dogs, whose size must preclude many of their admirers from keeping them.

Below: The Dobermann Pinscher was developed in Germany at the end of the nineteenth century specifically as a guard dog. Its ears are cropped abroad and it was therefore established in America, where cropping is allowed, much earlier than in Britain where cropping is banned. Modern dogs have a more easy-going temperament than the early imports.

Right: The German Shepherd is the most widely kept and versatile of all breeds. Like many breeds which have become very popular, poor temperament in some animals has given the breed an undeservedly bad reputation with some people. The majority of German Shepherds are dogs of integrity and intelligence, as is proved by their success in so many different fields.
Overleaf left: Greyhounds are amongst the oldest of purebred dogs. More are bred and kept for racing now than for any other purpose.
Overleaf right: Amongst the ten most popular breeds in America is the St Bernard. Giant dogs like this need a great deal of upkeep.

Far left: Few Afghans reached the Western world until the 1920s. Now the breed is known worldwide and most of the bloodlines stem from the original British imports. Their spectacular looks are adequate recompense for the time and care needed by that long coat.
Top left: A Beagle puppy has a beguiling, wide-eyed innocence.
Bottom left: An American Cocker showing the full glory of its adult coat.

Top left: The Basset Griffon Vendéen is a breed little known outside its native country, France.
Bottom left: The Miniature Schnauzer is one of the most popular of dogs in America and is well known in Britain and its homeland, Germany. The coat needs a good deal of trimming if the dog is to look smart.

Index

Acknowledgements

The publishers would like to thank the following organisations and individuals for their kind permission to reproduce the photographs in this book:

Antique Porcelain Company 12; Ardea (J. P. Fierraro) 32; Australian News and Information Bureau 76, 86; Barnaby's Picture Library 88, F.P.G. (Zimmermann) 91 above, (Richard Gee) 106 below, (Mike Jay) 35; S. C. Bisserot 24; Camera Press 89 below, 123, 154; Bruce Coleman 70, (H. Reinhard) 157 above; Colour Library International 54, 84–85, 153; Cooper Bridgeman Library 22, 23, (Roy Miles) 31; Anne Cumbers 11 below, 27, 28, 34, 36 above, 37, 38 above, 38 below, 40, 46, 48, 51 above, 64, 67, 69, 77 below, 83 above, 89 above, 92 above, 94, 105, 126 below, 131, 133, 134, 135, 136, 145, 158 above; Mary Evans Picture Library 9 right, 10; Robert Harding Associates 83 below; Michael Holford 9 left; Jacana (Soyamoto) 118 below, (B. Josedupont) 82, (Labat) 148; Keystone Press Agency 57 above; Mansell Collection 6; Jim Meads 119, 120–121, 124, 125; Jane Miller 16 below, 95 below; John Moss 51 below; Mike Peters 115; Pictor International 25, 49, 81, 93, 116–117, 126 above, 128 below, 155; Picturepoint 156; Dick Polak 143 above; Popperfoto 87, 151; John Rigby 147; RSPCA, courtesy A. J. Lennie 140; John Sims 68 below, 71; Spectrum Colour Library 2–3, 4, 26 above, 55, 62, 63 below, 113, 146, 158 below, (Tony Boxall) 47; Tony Stone Associates 58–59; Syndication International 101; Sally Anne Thompson 8, 11 above, 13, 14 above, 14 below, 16 above, 19 above, 19 below, 20, 21, 26 below, 29, 30, 36 above, 36 below, 41, 42 above, 42 below, 45 above, 45 below, 50, 53, 56, 61, 63 above, 66 above, 66 below, 68 above, 72, 75 above, 75 below, 77 above, 78 above, 78 below, 79 above, 79 below left, 79 below right, 92 below, 95 above, 96 above, 96 below, 98, 99, 100, 102, 103 above, 103 below, 104, 106 above, 107, 108 above, 108 below, 109, 110, 111, 114, 118 above, 122, 128 above, 130, 132, 138, 139, 141, 143 below, 150, 152, 157 below; Elizabeth Weiland 57 below; Barbara Woodhouse 52; ZEFA 149, (E. Deyle) 127, (J. Grossauer) 90, (R. Halin) 1, (E. Oechstein) 91 below, (Starfoto) 60.